ORGANISATIONAL STRUCTURE AND THE CARE OF THE MENTALLY RETARDED

Organisational Structure and the Care of the Mentally Retarded

Norma V. Raynes, Michael W. Pratt
and Shirley Roses

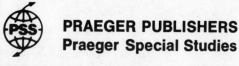

PRAEGER PUBLISHERS
Praeger Special Studies

New York • London • Sydney • Toronto

PRAEGER PUBLISHERS, PRAEGER SPECIAL STUDIES
383 Madison Avenue, New York, N.Y. 10017, U.S.A.

Published in the United States of America in 1979
by Praeger Publishers
A Division of Holt, Rinehart and Winston, CBS, Inc.

Library of Congress Catalog Card Number: 79-83740

Printed in Great Britain

CONTENTS

'There's no defined organisational structure here—it's chaos'
—An Assistant Superintendent.

'We have no authority'—A Unit Director.

'People don't want to recognise the Charge'—A Charge
Attendant.

'Nobody listens to us'—An Attendant.

'This is my home'—A Resident.

Postscript The Report of the Committee of Enquiry into Mental
Handicap Nursing and Care, Chairman Peggy Jay, published in March
1979, appeared too late for us to refer to it, but many of the findings
of the OPCS Survey commissioned by the Committee suggest that there
are similarities between the American establishments we describe and
their English counterparts.

PREFACE

Many people made the study described here possible. Perhaps we owe our greatest debt to our intellectual forefathers and our teachers: our ideas and skills grew out of the knowledge we had gained long before we formed an inter-disciplinary research team.

We owe much to the funding agency, the National Institute of Child Health and Human Development, whose grant from 1972 to 1974 made it possible for us to carry out such an extended study, and to Dr Hugo W. Moser who encouraged one of us to come to the United States to carry out the research. We owe thanks to members of the agencies of the Commonwealth of Massachusetts involved in the provision of services for the mentally retarded. Primarily but not exclusively this means the Department of Mental Health in the Commonwealth of Massachusetts; the Commissioners, the Assistant Commissioners of Mental Retardation; the Regional Administrators; the superintendents of the institutions; the Unit Directors, the direct care staff and the host of service personnel who allowed us access to the institutions and who for the most part tolerated our presence and questions with good humour. We owe a similar debt to the members of the various unions representing personnel in these institutions.

The three of us never failed to be impressed by the dignity and humour of the residents into whose homes we intruded. It is to them above all that this book is dedicated. How many of us would put up with research workers watching us all day? The direct-care workers were the other group of people who bore the brunt of our observations and questions. From them we received direct support on a daily basis throughout our field work, and without this the study could never have been completed.

Working with us for various periods over the three years were several people, including Suzanne Archigian, Garth Beattie, Lisa Boodman, Dennis Bumstead, Cassandra Hatjiandoniou, Justin Henry, Ilene Rubinstein, Margaret Weinberg. Some provided invaluable help with typing and clerical skills, others as field workers and analysts of data. We respect and appreciate the contribution each made to the study we here report.

Hillorie Applebaum, Katheryn Gabriella and Ilene Rubinstein helped with the collection and editing of material obtained from the residents quoted in Chapter 9.

Jane Keyes made helpful comments on an earlier version of this manuscript, and Margaret Adams, Sandra Barker, Caroline Godlove critically read various chapters for us. Janet Heath helped us with the typing of the bibliography and Gillian Andrews typed the remainder of the final manuscript and assisted with the compilation of the bibliography. We acknowledge our debt to their skill and patience.

We all owe our families gratitude for their tolerance of our absence from home on field trips, and for their help and understanding as we ploughed on, even after it was officially all over.

We know that what we have written here is ultimately our responsibility. We hope that what we have written disappoints no one who supported and encouraged us.

Norma V. Raynes
Michael W. Pratt
Shirley Roses
1979

Part One
BACKGROUND

1 INTRODUCTION

This book is an attempt to identify those features of large residential facilities for the mentally retarded which promote or inhibit individualised care. Our orientation is a sociological one and thus we have focused our attention on aspects of the organisation in which people live and work and not on the personalities of either those who provide care or those who receive it. The facilities we studied are commonly called institutions.

From a sociologist's perspective institutions for the mentally handicapped, or any other client group, are a sub-species of complex organisations. They have been labelled by Goffman (1961) as 'total institutions'. He defined these as 'a place of residence and work where large numbers of like-situated individuals . . . cut off from the wider society for an appreciative period of time, together lead an enclosed formally administered round of life' (p. 11). Many case studies of such places have been carried out (Stanton & Schwartz, 1954; Belknap, 1956; Caudill, 1958; Goffman, 1961; Salisbury, 1962; Polsky, 1963, to cite but a few). The limitations of the case study method applied to residential institutions have been well summarised by Tizard, Sinclair and Clarke (1975). In essence these studies assume, as does Goffman's theoretical work, that institutions are a unitary phenomenon, and imply that there are no differences either *between* or *within* them, which can be of consequence for those who live and work there. This assumption has been radically challenged by the findings of several comparative studies of large and small residential institutions. These comparative studies have used a multi-dimensional approach in their analysis of the characteristics of such settings. Wing & Brown (1970), and Ullman (1967) used it in their studies of mental hospitals, and Tizard (1975) in her study of residential nurseries. Millham, Bullock & Cherrett (1975) applied it in a study of approved schools as did Sinclair (1971) in his study of hostels for male probationers. In England, King, Raynes & Tizard (1971) adopted this approach in their study of residential facilities for mentally handicapped children. In that study, to which ours owes a great debt, King et al. (1971) developed a measure of care practices, the Child Management Scale, and showed that it is possible to measure differences in care in different settings. The development of such a measure has made systematic comparison of specific features of care practices possible and also

13

replicable and showed that it was possible to measure differences in care between institutions. This measure has been used in other studies carried out in the United States. McLain, Silverstein, Hubbell & Brownlees (1975) used it in a modified version in a study of one institution for the mentally handicapped in the United States to explore differences in management practices between living units within this institution. McCormick, Balla & Zigler (1975) report its application in a cross-national study of several American and Swedish residential facilities for the mentally handicapped. Both these studies reported measurable differences in the quality of care provided not only between but *within* institutions. King *et al.* (1971) also attempted to relate the differences they found in the quality of care in different settings to differences in the organisational structure of the settings at the level of the living units. They found differences between the hostels and the hospitals they studied. They also noted differences *within* these two types of residential facility but did not explore these intra-institutional differences.

We have tried to develop the work carried out by King *et al.* (1971) and others in a number of ways. We here summarise our endeavours.

1. We assume that care itself is a multi-dimensional phenomenon and that it is therefore possible to isolate and measure specific dimensions of the care-taking process, which can be shown to be different from those aspects of care covered in the Child Management Scale developed by King *et al.* (1971). To this end we have developed measures of the management of three areas of the living environment provided in the residential settings we studied.

2. We use a multi-dimensional approach in our study of the organisational structure of the settings in which care was provided. We followed the theoretical concepts developed by Pugh & Hickson and their colleagues (1963, 1968, 1969), Aiken & Hage (1966, 1967), and Hall (1962, 1963) in their studies of other types of complex organisations. We thus explore the extent to which formalisation and specialisation as well as centralisation are characteristic of these institutions at the residence level. With quantifiable measures of these dimensions we explore their effect on care practices and staff morale at the level of the residence.

3. We explore the interrelationship of the dimensions of organisation structure characterising the residences within the institutions.

4. We consider the contribution made by some of the personal attributes of care workers to their management of the residents.

5. We investigate the implications of dimensions of organisational

structure and personal staff characteristics at the level of individual staff performance in one area of their care-taking activities.

6. We attempt, less adequately we feel, to understand the way in which the several administrative levels in these institutions affect the organisation of the residences.

We have systematically attempted to explore differences within and between the institutional settings we studied on all these counts. From our data we have begun to build a model which takes account of the effect of a variety of organisational factors on care to provide information about which of these promote resident-oriented care. By this we mean care which is individualised and flexible.

We studied these factors in three large residential settings in one state in the United States. We suspect that much that we have found to be true in these places may well be true in others like them elsewhere in the United States and in England and in *smaller* (and currently more fashionable) residential facilities on both sides of the Atlantic. We do not know if our suspicions are justified. Perhaps other researchers will establish that. We have made developments in methodology and conceptual framework which we think will facilitate further comparative study and exploration of these issues.

We are well aware that institutions for the mentally retarded have had a bad press on both sides of the Atlantic. Often they have been justly berated for their inadequacies. Nirje (1969), Wolfensberger (1969, 1971), Blatt (1969), DHSS (1969), Morris (1969), Jones (1975), for example, have all provided ample evidence of the deficiencies of these settings. But it is not sufficient, if we are to improve the quality of residential services, whether these are large-scale institutions or smaller facilities, to cite their deficiencies or to write them off as incorrigible. Two hundred thousand people still live in the type of facility we worked in in the USA and about 50,000 live in comparable facilities in England (Scheerenberger, 1976; DHSS, 1977). A comparative multidimensional approach to these facilities can isolate specific factors contributing to institutional life. It can identify which facets of care are related to specific dimensions of the organisation's structure and characteristics of the personnel who work there. Such an approach does not assume that all aspects of care are equally affected by all dimensions of an organisation's structure, rather it assumes that these relationships have to be identified. We hope our approach will help those involved in making policy decisions and providing residential services for the mentally handicapped. As Tizard *et al.* (1975) have said, 'Inasmuch as we can describe those determining features of institutional life . . . we can begin to make rational choices between different ways of running institutions' (p. 1); and we can build environments which are free of features considered unacceptable.

We began this study in Massachusetts at a time when administrators of institutions for the mentally retarded were being told to institute major administrative changes in these facilities. The administrative changes were seen as a means of ameliorating conditions in large institutions. The warehouses, Miller & Gwynne (1972) have described, were to be transformed by administrative strategies into places where individualised, humane rather than custodial care could be practised. The administrative changes to be made were subsumed under the label unitisation, its major feature being the decentralisation of authority in previously centralised organisations. Such a solution could hardly be resisted by those who were left to run those unwanted and unloved places, despite evidence already accumulating which suggested that unit-isation was not necessarily a panacea for the problems of large resident-ial institutions. Most of this evidence was admittedly from studies of unitised mental hospitals, not facilities for the mentally retarded. Snow (1965) and Kiger (1966), for example, described some of the admin-istrative problems which were emerging in mental hospitals and the effects on staff morale. Shearn (1966) and English (1964) reported on the changes which had occurred in the definition of staff roles. Zubowicz (1967) raised questions about the extent to which unit directors' pro-posals were translated into policy at ward level. The existence of such cautionary evidence did not deter the Department of Mental Health in the Commonwealth of Massachusetts from making the implementation of unitisation mandatory in its state schools for the mentally retarded in 1969; and it was in such settings that our work was carried out. Initially, we did think of studying what was meant by unitisation and attempting to assess the effects of this administrative development by comparing a unitised with a non-unitised facility. However, the variance in the first institution we studied was so marked both in terms of the care provided and the organisational characteristics of the residences within it, that it would have been meaningless to have carried out a simple comparative study with a contrasting institution. Instead, we planned a study to enable us to ascertain whether the variance we found in organisational structure, staff attitudes and care practices were peculiar to this single institution or more generally characteristic of residential facilities of similar size and organisation. Our objective, in essence, was to understand what factors contributed to the differences we observed in the care provided for the residents in such settings, and specifically to identify those which were associated with individual care.

We have had some difficulty in writing this book because the terminology used in the United States is not always identical to that used in other countries and is not always readily interpreted. We have tried to explain what is meant by certain terms we use and to give their British equivalents. We use the terms mental retardation and mental handicap interchangeably. In America the facilities we studied are called state schools. They are known as mental subnormality hospitals in England. We refer to them sometimes by their proper names, sometimes we call them residential facilities, often we call them institutions. In these residential facilities the living units are known as buildings. We use this name interchangeably with the term residence. We refer to the mentally handicapped people who live there as the residents or clients. We hope our decision to use American and English terminology interchangeably in some instances will not confuse the reader. We know that the titles are different but the contents are the same.

The book is divided into six parts. In Part One the background to the study is discussed, and we include a brief description of the structure of services for the mentally retarded in Massachusetts, the State in which the research was carried out. Part Two focuses on research methods, and can be ignored by those uninterested in technical details of the construction of measures and of data collection. In Part Three we describe in detail the people of these places, the residents and their staff. Part Four describes the care we found to be provided in these settings in terms of the management of daily events; the speech used by direct-care staff to residents; the physical environment; and contact with the surrounding community. In this section we use material provided for one of us (NVR) by the residents because it clearly illustrates the residents' views on a world we have tried to describe and quantify. Perhaps our research findings may result in changes these writers would approve of. We hope so.

[The residents were asked to contribute material for an anthology. A grant by the Joseph P. Kennedy Jnr Foundation (to NVR) facilitated the collection of this material. Although the anthology was never published, permission to print the material was legally obtained from the residents.]

In Part Five we are concerned with the question why the differences in care, reported in Part Four, exist. We thus consider the effect on care practices of the characteristics of staff and residents and various dimensions of the organisational structure. We also explore the implications for care of the interrelationship of various dimensions of the organisation's structure. Finally, in Part Six we summarise our findings and spell out what we think their implications are for those who provide residential services.

Summary

We have tried to show how complex are the facilities we call institutions. We have learnt in the course of our research that there are many myths about them. We are totally convinced that there are no single-factor solutions to the abundance of problems and deficiencies which we, like others before us, found characterise large residential facilities. Tizard *et al.* (1975) have argued a strong case for identifying the distinctive features of institutional life. Not least among the reasons they cite is the need to promote policies based on sound comparative evidence. Zigler (1976) recently said:

> the mental retardation field is in a state of flux and disarray. Some years ago, experts convinced decision makers that special education was the solution to the problem of training the retarded. This view is now suspect and decision makers are committing themselves to such concepts as normalisation and deinstitutionalisation. I . . . view these concepts as little more than slogans that are badly in need of an empirical data base. We have little knowledge about what is the best type of classroom or the optimal institutional setting for the retarded. (p. 52)

We wholeheartedly concur with his sentiments.

We hope that those who struggle to read our inevitably inadequate summaries of the complexity of these residential facilities will glean some insights from their reading. We trust that the planners and administrators will get some help in their understanding of what it is in these places that could promote better services for the mentally retarded.

2 THE GEOGRAPHICAL AND ADMINISTRATIVE CONTEXT OF THE STUDY

The Commonwealth of Massachusetts is a state of some five-and-a-half million people, and 8,257 square miles. It has a number of commercial and industrial centres and large rural sections. At the time we carried out our study, it had five large residential establishments for its retarded residents which were run by the Commonwealth. Four of these were called state schools and one of them was called a state hospital. At the commencement of this study one of these was involved in a class action suit, a legal action brought against the facility by the parents of its clients, and another was being reorganised administratively. After visiting these two facilities we decided that they had enough problems of their own, without having to meet the demands of our research team, and we therefore concentrated our activities in the remaining three establishments.

The Commonwealth is divided into seven administrative regions, which were established by law in 1966 to facilitate the operation of the Department of Mental Health, the state's governmental department with statutory responsibility for providing services for the mentally retarded. Each region had both an administrator for mental health and an administrator for mental retardation. The relationship between these two officers was not clearly defined, nor was their relationship to the Commissioner for Mental Health and the Assistant Commissioner for Mental Retardation. The Commissioners' offices were in the state-wide Department of Mental Health, which was located in Boston, the political and administrative capital of the Commonwealth. In principle, the Central Office — as the office of the Commissioner and the Assistant Commissioner was called — would operate through the regional administrators. In practice, as we observed, directives could and did arrive on the desk of the superintendents of the institutions directly from the Central Office as well as from the regional administrators. During the course of our study, two Assistant Commissioners for Mental Retardation came and went, and the Commissioner for Mental Health himself was replaced. The appointment of the Commissioner was made by the Governor of the Commonwealth.

In addition to the Department of Mental Health and its regional offices, several other departments operating in the Commonwealth were

19

involved in the running of facilities we studied. Within the Commonwealth there were a number of other human service departments, each
with their own Commissioner and budget. During the course of our
study a Department of Human Services was established, which in theory
was an umbrella department accountable for the activities of all the
departments in the state which provided services for those of the Commonwealth's citizens who had special needs. There was much conflict
and competition between these several departments, the Department of
Human Services, and the Department of Administration and Finance.
The impact of these wider administrative systems on the day-to-day
activities of the institutions deserves detailed study. Our data collected
about them was obtained from the vantage point of institutional personnel, however, and we have chosen to limit our discussion of these matters
to a minimum, chiefly because our information about them is decidedly
partial.

All the state schools we studied also had some affiliation with local
universities, often providing practicum placements for students training
in neurology, psychiatry, psychology, social work and so on. The needs
and goals of these students and the universities from which they came
were often very different from the needs of the residents and the goals
of the staff who worked in the facilities. Captive populations can be
good PhD thesis material, as well as sources of research data for people
like ourselves.

Thus the institutions were an integral part of a complex set of relationships involving competing participants with varying degrees of power
and influence. The parents, the media, the courts and the employee
unions all contributed as well to the pressures which operated on the
administrators charged with the day-to-day responsibility for running
these establishments. In short, they were by no means islands entire
unto themselves, nor were their superintendents possessors of anything
like absolute power. A day spent in the offices of any of the superintendents, listening to the phone calls they received, let alone discussing
the contents of their mail, would make it clear to anyone that these men
and women worked under a great number of pressures and constraints
which emanated from many and various sources outside the institution.

All these institutions had been unitised, the first two in 1969. This
pattern of administrative reorganisation was made possible by the politicians' approval of the establishment of a number of new unit director
positions to be allocated to the institutions. What this administrative
reorganisation meant in practice we discuss in Chapter 13. In principle,
the unit directors were to co-ordinate and plan, with the aid of a team

of professional and direct-care staff, the services and programmes for the individual residents.

Since several unit directors were to be appointed, this meant that the residents could be grouped into units on the basis of certain criteria. In the settings we worked in, the units were described as functional units, and the residents in them were assumed to have common needs because of their level of ability, age and sex. The units were given names which were said to indicate their functions or goals, for instance the Adult Training Unit. Schreiber (1976), describing the role of the social worker in unitised institutions, noted that 'unitisation has been welcomed by some people, it has bewildered others, and it has threatened some individuals' (p. 23). It seemed to us, as we tried to understand the work of people in these settings, that unitisation did have all the consequences that Schreiber mentioned. It also seemed to us that in practice unit-isation was interpreted in many different ways, which we discuss in Chapter 13. It is perhaps not surprising that unitisation should not turn out to be the simple form described in the planners' handbook, *Massachusetts Plans for its Retarded* (1966). Any attempt to introduce administrative reorganisation of a structure which involves a shift in power is bound to run into problems. This is particularly so in complex organisations with long-established departments, the directors of which are not only concerned with maintaining the power they have, but are supported in this endeavour by their long-established links with state-wide administrative systems as well as with each other. The problems generated by introducing new managerial positions into such long-established systems, to which in theory a great deal of authority is to accrue, are not solved overnight or even after two or three years, as we discovered.

It was in this context that we began our attempt to study the organ-isational features of these state schools, the characteristics of the people who worked in them, and the care they provided for their residents.

Part Two

DATA COLLECTION AND MEASUREMENT TECHNIQU

3 THE RESIDENTS AND THEIR CARE

As we have already indicated, the analysis of the data collected in one large residential facility clearly demonstrated that there was much variance both in the care provided there and in the institution's organisational structure. The data suggested that there were relationships between certain aspects of the organisation's structure and the range in care practices found within it and we became concerned with the further exploration of these relationships. To examine them we selected four residences in two other institutions. These two institutions, like the first, had been unitised and thus it was within such settings, comparable in terms of their formal organisation, that we carried out our research. In this chapter and the next we discuss the ways in which we examined the areas of institutional life which became the focus of the study, and provide the background to our choice of these areas.

Resident Characteristics

Let us begin with the residents. The research literature is conflicting in the evidence so far presented on the effect of the residents' characteristics on care-taking behaviour. (King et al., 1971; Kushlick 1975; McCormick et al., 1975.) There is, however, a fairly consistent literature in social psychology which points to the importance of situational determinants of behaviour. (Milgram, 1965; Zimbardo, Haney & Banks, 1975; Mischel, 1973.) These studies and others have indicated how personality and individual differences pale as determinants of social behaviour when compared with the situation at hand. It seemed to us that a useful way of conceptualising the characteristics of the residents would be as an important determinant of the work which had to be carried out in the residences. We collected data on the number of residents and their daily living skills (whether they could feed, wash, and dress themselves for example), their academic abilities (for example, reading and writing), their daily activities and their behaviour problems. We developed an interview based on a questionnaire used by Kushlick, Blunden & Cox (1973) to collect these data from the direct-care staff working on the wards. We chose to get our data in this fashion for two reasons. First, in the large residences we did not expect the building heads to be able to give us the detailed information we required. Secondly, we planned three other interviews with the building heads, which we knew would take at least three hours of their time. We supplemented the data about the residents thus obtained from the institutions' central files. From these sources we obtained data on the age, sex and IQ of the residents. We did not attempt to assess the reliability of the interview since this had been done previously by one of us (NVR) in a study of the whole population of one of the institutions. At that time two direct-care staff in each ward were asked to complete the same questionnaire on each resident. The reliability coefficients obtained in this study ranged from .70 to .84 for the items on the questionnaire. Because of time constraints we were unable to carry out independent assessments of the residents' IQ. We tried to establish some indication of the validity of the data collected from institution records by examining the relationship between the quotient obtained from the records and our data on the residents' social and academic skills collected as described above. We found high correlations between IQ and the residents' daily living skills and academic performance, the correlations being between 0.7 and 0.9, but not between IQ and behaviour disorders. We thus chose to use resident IQ as a summary measure of functional ability. We use this quotient, in our explorations of the effect of residents' ability on care provided, rather than the detailed data on reported performance. IQ, in short, became one of the situational factors which we hypothesised might influence the direct-care staff's care-taking behaviour.

Dimensions of Care

We were, as we have noted, concerned to establish how the residents were cared for. To do this we chose to examine four dimensions of care. We think that just as it is possible to conceptualise an organisation's structure as a series of dimensions (Pugh *et al.*, 1963), so can one productively apply this analytical approach to resident care. Each of these dimensions may vary independently and each area of resident management which they represent may be differentially affected by the organisation's structure and the characteristics of the staff and residents.

King *et al.* (1971), in their study of retarded children in residential care, operationalised some of the attributes described by Goffman (1961) as characteristic of staff/inmate interaction in total institutions. These researchers argued that care could be thought of as a continuum along which practices could be seen to vary. The two ends of this continuum they labelled child-oriented and institution-oriented. We think that these polarities can be used to label the extremes of other forms of interaction which occur between staff and residents in the provision of care for the latter, in addition to those situations of daily life that are included in the scale they developed and applied in their study. We therefore attempted to look at other aspects of care, including staff talk to residents, the provision of physical amenities, and the residents' involvement in community activities. We discuss each of these four measures in turn and then describe their interrelationship.

Data on staff/resident interaction in recurring daily events and other social situations were collected following the protocols established by King *et al*. (1971). We were unable to collect data on the proportion of time the residents spent in leisure activities, and the item on the original scale concerning the way in which staff helped residents with their toileting was not applicable to the adult population we studied. We therefore dropped these two items and used 28 of the original 30 items only. We refer to this abbreviated scale as the Revised Resident Management Practices Scale (RRMP). To obtain data for the scale, staff in charge of the buildings (building heads) were interviewed about the management of daily events; for example, the time residents were awakened, or how their birthdays were recognised. We had some initial doubts about selecting this person as our informant, but a pilot study in which the building head and direct-care staff working on specific wards were both interviewed indicated that we could expect to get reasonably accurate information from the building heads about the management of the events covered in the scale. A second reason for doing this was the lack of consistency between the residences in the way in which direct-care staff were deployed. Some staff did work on particular wards, but in other cases different staff were assigned to different dormitories on different days. Data for some of the items on this scale have to be collected using observational techniques, namely residents' activities between getting up and breakfast, the management of their meal times and showering. Inter-interviewer and inter-observer reliabilities for this scale were both in the .80s. The data collected were scored according to the procedure defined by King *et al.* (1971). For each of the 28 items, a score of 0 was assigned if the information indicated that the practices were resident-oriented and a score of 2 if they were institutionally oriented. A score of 1 was given if a mixed resident-and-institution-oriented practice was indicated by the data. The 28 items thus gave a possible range of scores from 0 to 56, the lower score indicating maximally resident-oriented care practices. The 28-item scale which is reproduced in Appendix 2.1 correlated +0.96 with the original 15-item version of the measure described by King & Raynes (1968). This first version was shown by King and his colleagues (1971) to correlate +0.92 with the 30-

item version they used in their study of residential settings for mentally retarded children.

Our choice of staff speech as a second dimension of care practices was based on research evidence indicating that verbal stimulation promotes linguistic growth in normal development, e.g. Bayley, Rhodes, Gooch & Marc (1971). The feasibility of collecting data in this area had recently been shown by the work of Barbara Tizard, and her colleagues (1972). Their work, while carried out in residential nurseries for normal children, gave us a framework in which to develop this second measure of the care provided for the residents.

Tizard, Cooperman, Joseph & Tizard (1972) had coded staff language to children into three major categories. First, they designated as inform- ative speech that which offered opinion, information, or explanation. Second, they classified as controlling speech statements which gave orders without explanation. In their third category, they subsumed perfunctory comment, like 'hello' and 'goodbye'. They also used several other categories which we did not attempt to explore in this study. Their work was the basis of both the recording instrument we used and the categorisation of data for purposes of analysis. We collected the data by observing all direct-care staff and building heads on duty in each residence for a period of two hours, from the beginning of the evening meal onwards. We repeated these observations on two different days. Each member of staff was observed for five minutes in random rotation. Within each period, five consecutive time samples of ten seconds of their speech were obtained, followed by 50 seconds for recording. In this fifty-second period, the first sentence in the preceding ten-second interval was recorded verbatim. It was then coded into one of the three categories of speech designed to describe the function of the sentence in relation to the residents. The first category was informative speech — that is, statements which explain, give new information, or ask the residents for information. The second category, controlling speech, was subdivided into positive control and negative control. The former were statements which requested that a resident begin an activity, the latter that he terminate an activity. We condensed all other speech into our third category, 'other talk'. Where no speech was observed, we recorded this observation in a separate 'no talk' category. We also recorded for each interval: the location of the interaction by room, whether the resident spoken to replied during the observation interval, whether other staff were present in the room, the status of these staff *vis-à-vis* the speaker, and finally the approximate number of residents present in the room.

Five observers were involved in the data collection. Reliability studies were carried out throughout the field work. Two observers independently recorded and coded simultaneously for two hours of observation in each study. A total sample of 612 observation periods was obtained to rate inter-observer reliability in seven of the residences. Coefficients of concordance were computed for the major language codes and the other data classified during the recording period. The average agreement on language codes was +0.88. This compares favourably with the Tizard *et al.* (1972) reports of +0.80 in their study. The overall coefficient of concordance for each of the major language codes was +0.65 for negative control statements; +0.95 for positive control statements; +0.91 for informative speech, and +0.85 for 'other talk'. For the other data, co-efficients ranged from +0.85 to +0.97. We also assessed the stability of these speech measures by correlating each building's score with itself over observational 'days' 1 and 2. This correlation was 0.71 for informative speech, suggesting acceptable stability in our measures.

From these data we developed a summary measure of the quality of staff speech to residents. We have called this measure the Informative Speech Index (ISI). This index was obtained by computing the average proportion of all observations which included speech classified as informative, eliminating all those periods when no residents were present at all. The range of possible scores on this measure is therefore from 0 to 100 per cent. We think of low scores on this measure as describing an institution-oriented approach to the management of residents, as compared to a high score, which indicates a resident-centred approach to care by staff.

In the collection of data for this measure, a notation was made designating the individual staff member being observed. This subsequently enabled us to relate individual staff members' performance on this measure to other characteristics of the workers we observed. The ISI was computed as an aggregate for all staff in the building, but the existence of individual records also enabled us to test our observations against individual performance values.

The third dimension of care we examined was the physical environment provided in the residences. We think the physical environment of a residence can itself provide a source of sensory stimulation or deprivation. It can also undermine programmes designed to promote growth and development, by failing for example to provide personalised storage facilities or privacy, as where toilets are without doors or partitions and showers without cubicles or curtains. Only Morris (1969) in England has systematically studied the environment and amenities provided in residential settings for the retarded. She showed not only variation between the hospitals in her survey, but also between wards in the same hospital. Wards without storage facilities for individuals, living rooms which are spartan and lacking in tables and chairs, and residences where recreational materials are non-existent, do not provide environments in which stimulating and resident-centred management can easily occur. Levy & McLeod (1977) report beneficial results of experimental changes in the physical environment of a ward in an American institution, but we do not know of any other American study which systematically examines this aspect of resident care. The Joint Commission on Accreditation of Hospitals (1971) has set out minimum standards with regard to bed space and provision of toilets. We were not able to measure directly the cubic footage per resident, though in some of the residences we surveyed it was clear that it would not have been possible to fit bedside lockers without drastic rearrangement of the available space to accommodate beds. What we tried to do was to collect information about the physical environment in terms of the numbers of residents who were required to use basic facilities like bedrooms, bathrooms, handbasins and showers (giving us some indication of the measure of 'overcrowding') and the availability of furniture which would permit more personalised care, such as lockers, wardrobes, toilets with doors and partitions. We also tried to get some data on aspects of the furnishings which would add to the non-institutional quality of these residences and might make them more homely. We therefore looked for curtains and rugs in the bedrooms and living rooms, as well as for mirrors in bathrooms and pictures on the walls. Thus we combined in one measure some of the features of the environment in which the residents lived which Morris (1969) called 'basic provisions' and those she referred to as 'amenities'. We did not, with the exception of an item on the presence of televisions, attempt to establish what materials were available for recreational purposes.

We collected our data by walking round each of the residences, checklist in hand, noting the presence or absence and numbers of each aspect of the physical environment that was on our list. The checklist included 30 items. An item analysis of these data was carried out, and 22 items met the criteria for inclusion in a scale, as defined in Maxwell (1971). Each of these 22 items was scored on a five-point rating scale. Each feature of the physical environment was computed either as a percentage or a ratio. Percentages were used where features of a particular room were being examined, for example the percentage of bedrooms with rugs or carpets. Ratios were used where the availability of an item for individual residents was of concern, for example the ratio of bedrooms to residents, or wardrobes to residents. The scores assigned to the items expressed as percentages ranged from four where less than 20 per cent of the rooms had the amenity, decreasing for every 20 per cent to 0 where these amenities were present in four-fifths or more of the rooms. The scores for items expressed as ratios were as follows:

Ratios	Score
1:1 - 1:2	0
1:3 - 1:5	1
1:6 - 1:10	2
1:11 - 1:15	3
1:16 +	4

The scores obtained for each of these items were added to provide a total score for each of the residences. This measure we refer to as our Index of the Physical Environment (IPE). The possible range of scores was 0 to 88, the higher score indicating low levels of provision in the physical environment.

Our fourth measure of care provided for residents concerned the extent to which they were in contact with the community beyond the confines of the institution. It is true that these places are total institutions, but they are not legally defined as ones in which the residents have to be deprived of contact with the host community. One of the major critic- isms of such institutions has been the extent to which they do deprive their residents of 'normal' activities, available only outside their confines, like visits to a cinema, a museum, a shopping expedition, or a neighbour's house, as well as contact with parents. To the extent that these experiences are denied to the residents, their care would indeed seem to be institution- oriented. Balla (1976), reviewing research in this area, does not report any systematic study of such types of involvement in the community other than contact with parents, although he notes that a recurring criticism of institutions is their isolated location which makes contact with the outside world difficult. It is clearly possible to quantify the extent to which community facilities are used by the staff in their man- agement of the residents. To do this we obtained data from the building heads by means of an interview. We asked them to give us the names of all residents going into the surrounding community in the last month to participate in a number of activities. For example we asked them who had been to a cinema, or the hairdresser, or on an overnight visit. The responses to these questions were computed as a percentage of all the residents in the building, and this percentage was scored on a five-point rating scale. A score of 0 was assigned where 80 to 100 per cent of the residents were involved in the activity, a score of 1 where 60 to 80 per cent were involved, a score of 2 where 40 to 60 per cent were involved and scores of 3 and 4 respectively to items where 20-40 per cent or 0-20 per cent were involved in these activities. The scores for each item included in the index on the basis of an item analysis were summed to give an overall score for residence. The possible range of scores was 0 to 48, the former score indicating that all the residents had been involved in each activity in the community within the last month. The latter score indicated that no resident from the building had taken part in any of the community-based activities asked about in this period. We call this measure the Index of Community Involvement.

Relationships among Indices of Care

We have just described how we developed and used four separate indices of the quality of care for each residence: a measure of daily event management (the RRMP), a measure of staff speech (the ISI), a measure of the physical environment (the IPE), and a measure of community contact (the ICI). As we have pointed out, we believe that these measures tapped independent aspects of the care provided for the residents. We were able to establish the extent to which the four measures were independent of each other, and to that extent assess the validity of the concept that care can be viewed as a series of dimensions. We found that all these measures were correlated with the residents' IQ, the significance of which we discuss in Chapter 10. Here we need only note that the effect of this factor had to be partialled out to assess properly the interdependence of these four measures of care. Because the RRMP was a previously established scale, we focused on it in an evaluation of the other measures. The RRMP, for our 21 residences, turned out to be significantly associated only with the ICI — as shown in Table 3.1.

Table 3.1: Intercorrelations of Care Measures
Partial r's (controlled for IQ)

	ISI	*IPE*	*ICI*
RRMP	- .23	+ .05	+ .56
ISI	—	- .42*	- .11
IPE	—	—	+ .13

* p $<$ .05, one-tailed

These two scales are relatively highly correlated, suggesting that the measurement of daily events reflected in the RRMP is not greatly amplified by information regarding the residents' contact with the community. If care on the RRMP is institution-oriented, contact with the community is invariably restricted for the residents. However, when care is resident-oriented, community contact is sometimes quite extensive, though not always so.

There is no relationship, with IQ controlled, between the ISI and the RRMP. These two measures appear to tap distinctive aspects of care. Other dimensions of our language observations, however, were related to the RRMP (see Pratt, Bumstead & Raynes, 1976 for a more extensive discussion). For example, the incidence of controlling speech in the residence was correlated + .40 with the RRMP score with IQ controlled (p<.05, one-tailed). This indicates that institution-oriented buildings are more likely to be characterised by a higher frequency of orders to the residents, a quite predictable association. The frequency of informative speech, however, appears to measure a separate dimension of care.

What about the relation between our measure of the physical environment (the IPE) and the RRMP? Again, as Table 3.1 indicates, it appears that these two scales are independent, once average building IQ is controlled. However, the IPE is substantially associated with our speech index. This relation indicates that an impoverished physical environment is moderately correlated with less informative staff/resident interaction styles. The pattern of these data suggests that lack of individualised amenities (e.g., own bedrooms, mirrors) was particularly strongly associated with less informative interaction in the residences. It seems not unreasonable to suggest that certain features of a more stimulating physical environment could directly induce a more conversational interchange between staff and residents. While we have no firm basis for testing this reasonable hypothesis with the present correlational data, Levy & McLeod's (1977) experimental work lends some support to this line of reasoning. Their introduction of physical changes into a ward to enrich its environment did promote socially and psychologically desirable improvements in behaviour.

In Chapter 8, we will provide a descriptive report of the results for all four of our measures of care – their meaning in terms of the lives of the residents. However, in our subsequent analyses of the factors affecting care-taking, we will focus on the RRMP and the ISI only. We do this for two reasons. First, these two dimensions of care are independent of one another, yet both directly reflect the activities of the daily care-taking staff. The ICI is strongly related to the RRMP and thus, in one sense, somewhat redundant. The IPE, though independent of the RRMP, does not measure features of the environment which derive in any direct sense from the direct-care staff. In general, it makes no sense theoretically or logically to examine the effect of organisational structure or staff attitudes on the availability of toilets to residents, since these staff are powerless to effect changes in this situation.

A second reason for narrowing our focus to two care measures is our attempt to impose some clarity on the complexity of our findings. Two outcome measures of care seem just about enough to handle within the context of the multiplicity of other variables considered in the study. These two measures of care represent areas of direct-care staff activity which could be modified if change was thought to be desirable. In the next chapter, we describe how we went about studying the factors affecting care in these residential settings.

4 THE STAFF

Theoretical Background

Pugh and his colleagues (1963, 1968), studying a wide range of industrial and tertiary organisations, argued that Weber's ideal type construct of bureaucracy was limited as an analytical tool in the study of complex organisations. Such an ideal type presupposes the coexistence of all the attributes it defines as characteristic of bureaucracy. These researchers found it more useful to conceptualise each of the component characteristics as dimensions of an organisation's structure and to attempt to establish empirically the extent to which each dimension was present in an organisation. Weber's ideal type enabled them to identify the component parts of a bureaucratic organisation, and each of these was then operationally defined. We found Pugh & Hickson's approach particularly useful in trying to study the complex web of roles and their interrelationships which comprised the structure of the organisations we were studying.

We focused on four dimensions of the organisational structure of the three institutions, in which the staff worked and the residents lived. These are: centralisation, formalisation, communication and specialisation. Before we discuss the factors influencing our decision to study these four dimensions, we give our operational definitions of them. By centralisation we mean the extent to which authority is delegated. Formalisation we define as the extent to which rules and written regulations constrain the tasks carried out by workers in these settings. By communication we refer to the frequency of opportunity for information exchange between staff involved directly with the care of the residents and other groups of staff. Specialisation we define as the degree to which the task of caring for people is split up into parts and the parts allocated to different kinds of staff.

Our reasons for choosing to focus on these four aspects of the organisations' structure were several, and we shall briefly review them here. We first set out to describe the characteristics of the structure of an organisation that had been unitised. In the planners' and administrators' description of these structures (Massachusetts Mental Retardation Planning Project, 1966; Greenblatt & Stone, 1972) the notion of decentralisation of authority was basic. We had naïvely assumed that within one institution there would be consistency in the perceptions by staff at the

same level regarding the extent of decentralisation. As we have already
pointed out, early in the study we discovered that this was not the case.
Within one institution there was considerable difference in the extent to
which staff working in the various residences saw authority as being
delegated. We noted that other researchers, Hall (1967), and Paulson
(1974), for example, had recorded the beneficial consequences of decentralisation of decision making in a variety of organisational settings,
including health care institutions. Paulson's study examined the interrelationship between centralisation and other structural dimensions and
the effectiveness of several organisations which he defined as degree of
perceived goal attainment. He found that effectiveness increased as
centralisation decreased. His study and others had compared one setting
with another. Just as differences across organisations might be attributable to variations on this dimension in their structure, so might variations
within them.

A few studies concerned with the degree of centralisation in residential settings for the mentally retarded had shown this factor to be significant in accounting for differences in the care-taking characteristic of the
settings. King *et al.* (1971) had found that the care of retarded children
in residential settings was more resident-oriented where those in daily
charge of the living units frequently participated in several aspects of
the decision-making process. Holland (1973), utilising the index of
care developed by Raynes & King (1968), studied residences in an
institution for both retarded children and adults. He found that the unit
directors' perception of the extent to which the residences in their units
were decentralised was related to the type of care practice in the residence.
The greater the extent of decentralisation of these residences, the more
resident-oriented were the staffs' care-taking behaviours. Tizard *et al.*
(1972) studied residential nurseries for pre-school children, using as a
measure of care practices the speech used by staff to the children (the
measure from which our ISI was derived). Tizard *et al.* (1972) found that
in nurseries where the staff perceived themselves to have more authority
over aspects of the day-to-day management of the living units, the staff
used stimulating 'informative' speech more frequently than did staff in
nurseries where authority was perceived to be highly centralised.

These three studies are relatively consistent in suggesting that decentralisation is positively related to the provision of resident-centred care. Two
of the studies compared different settings on this dimension and one
(Holland) examined living units within one setting. The latter approach
suggests that differences in decentralisation *within* a setting may well
account for some of the variance found in care practices within it. However,

none of these studies measured the direct-care workers' perceptions of centralisation or the relationship of these to care. Either the head of the residence staff or of the larger administrative unit (Holland's study) was interviewed. Direct-care staff comprise the largest group of staff in US institutions (Scheerenberger, 1965). Simply on this account the significance of their perceptions of the organisation in which they work ought to be explored. In addition, of course, they are the staff most directly involved in providing care. Without assessing the perceptions of direct-care workers themselves, we cannot understand how the apparently beneficial effects of decentralisation are mediated. Thus, given the existing evidence of the contribution of decentralisation to the quality of care provided, we sought to establish how decentralisation was perceived by the unit directors, the building heads, and the direct-care staff, and to explore the implications of these perceptions for the care-taking process. Centralisation has been shown by other workers to have significance for the morale of staff in organisations, too. Tannenbaum & Masarik (1950) found a positive association between high staff morale and decentralised authority. Aiken & Hage's (1966) findings of an association between a high degree of centralisation and high levels of worker alienation support the earlier research, although the measures they used were different.

Aiken & Hage's (1966) work included an analysis of the interrelationship of dimensions of organisational structure and their implications for worker morale. Thus they examined the extent to which the organisations they studied were formalised, and found that the presence of many rules and regulations was also associated with low morale amongst workers. Morale was measured by them in terms of worker satisfaction, both with work tasks and with co-workers. These two indicators of morale, though conceptually distinguishable, were found to be highly intercorrelated. We have not encountered, in any empirical study of residential facilities for the retarded, an examination of the implications of formalisation on the organisation's structure. Studies of worker morale in these settings have suggested that a lack of opportunities to use initiative, as well as problems with superiors, are strongly associated with worker alienation and high turnover, as noted by Minge & Bowman (1969). A lack of opportunity to use initiative may well derive from the presence of a high degree of formalisation as well as centralisation.

Formalisation may also act as an inhibiting factor in the provision of individualised care, as well as lowering staff morale. The constraints of formal written rules and regulations and of job descriptions could reduce the flexibility the care staff need in order to provide care adapted to the needs of different residents in differing situations. Grusky (1959) noted that the absence of formal rules in a therapeutically oriented prison legitimised relatively individualised relationships between staff and inmates. Blau (1970) has argued that formalisation of procedures impedes flexibility of practice. However, in his own study of the operation of government social security agencies in the US, he found that decentralisation of authority was associated with a high level of formalisation. In interpreting these findings, he argued that the more detailed and extensive are the rules defining staff activity, the more feasible is the delegation of authority. By contrast, Paulson (1974) found that low levels of formalisation were associated with decentralisation and high levels of communication, and so the existing evidence on this point is conflicting.

Communication may be an alternative means of monitoring activity in situations where decentralisation is high. The importance of communication between personnel at the same level in non-routine task situations has been noted by Perrow (1972). Resident-oriented care, as we have defined it, is by implication a non-routine way of dealing with the residents. It would seem that individual-oriented care practices could best be maintained by frequent contact between the various shifts in the building. It might also be enhanced by communication between direct-care staff and other personnel involved in planning and in the implementation of programmes and activities designed for the residents. Etzioni (1960) has presented evidence to show that increased frequency of group discussion increases subordinates' support of new activities, and the importance of communication for effective care has been emphasised in many studies of mental hospitals (e.g., Stanton & Schwartz, 1954; Caudill, 1958). Thus, research in settings other than institutions for the retarded suggested to us the importance of considering the organisational dimensions of formalisation and communication as potentially important factors affecting the provision of care and worker morale.

The study by King and his colleagues (1971) examined the extent to which residential organisations varied in the degree to which the division of labour was specialised. They found that where the division of labour among direct-care staff and building heads was highly specialised, care was institution-oriented. Henry's (1957) theoretical paper on the structure and function of human service organisations provides us with some ideas as to why the relationship described by King *et al.* should exist. Where all the care-taking tasks to be completed are carried

out by a single individual, Henry suggests that workers are highly
motivated and can plan on an individual basis for all aspects of the
client's care. In his theoretical formulation, Henry further links the
nature of the authority system and specialisation in the division of labour,
noting that in what he describes as 'simple undifferentiated subordination',
i.e. where a worker who is responsible for all the tasks involved in caring
for a client has a single supervisor, communication is clearer and the
worker feels supported. At any rate, the empirical findings of King *et al.*
regarding the dangers of over-specialisation, unique in the literature on
the care of the retarded, seemed to us to be important enough to merit
replication.

Following Pugh *et al.* (1963), we have thus conceived of the structure
of the organisations we studied in terms of a number of dimensions. This
enables us to try independently to explore the implications of each
aspect of an organisation's structure for the care provided. It may be
that different organisational dimensions are of varying significance for
different aspects of care. From a practical point of view for those interest-
ed in improving care, such information should be of more use than know-
ing that some global phenomenon, e.g. the organisation of an institution
or its administration, was a factor affecting care. There is a second benefit
to this approach, we think, for it permits the examination of the inter-
relation between each aspect of the structure itself. Ultimately it should
enable us to move towards the development of a model of the dimensions
of an organisation's structure and the consequences of these and their
interrelationships for different aspects of residential care.

Using these analytical concepts required that we develop empirically
based measures of them. Our attempts to do this at the upper administrative levels of the institutions were not as extensive as we would have
liked. Our data on the dimensions of the organisation as they relate to the
chief executives, the department heads, and the unit directors remain
essentially at a descriptive level. We had neither the time nor the resources to go much beyond semi-structured interviewing of members of
these groups. Therefore, in our account of the organisations' structure
as it relates to these upper administrative levels, we can only present
summary descriptive material and suggest how the organisation of these
positions and strata in the institutions are likely to be significant for the
organisational structure of the residences. It is the views and perceptions
of the residence staff on which we have focused most of our data collection effort, as described below.

Measures of Organisational Structure

In the residences we differentiated between two levels of staff: the charge attendants, building heads or supervisors as we call them, and the attendants or direct-care staff, the building heads' immediate subordinates. We asked all the direct-care staff in the residences to complete a questionnaire and return it to us. In this we asked for information about their participation in several types of decisions relating to their work. From responses to three questions, we derived our measure of the workers' perception of centralisation. Direct-care staff were also asked to indicate whether they had received: (*a*) a job description, and (*b*) written rules and regulations relating to the carrying out of their work. Responses to these two questions were substantially correlated over the sample ($r = + 0.45$, $p < .01$) and we therefore thought it reasonable to combine them into a single index of formalisation. From responses to questions about the frequency of meetings with direct-care workers on other shifts, unit directors, and professional staff we derived indices of the perception of communication with different groups of colleagues. We developed a measure of staff morale from responses to a question about the helpfulness of co-workers. We also obtained a measure of their general concern for resident needs from their responses to two open-ended questions about their work. One of these questions was: 'What do you find to be the main problems in doing your job?', and the other asked 'Are there any changes you would like to see here?' We categorised the responses to these questions into two groups; the first being those which indicated the presence of a general concern for the residents. Comments thus classified included those where the needs of the residents for more programmes, better treatment, or more freedom were mentioned—for example, 'I would like to see a family care or cottage system to meet the needs of the residents.' In the other category we placed comments which did not include direct reference to the residents' needs. For example, 'There is a lack of *real* communication through the chain of command. The leaders could make an honest effort to assist us.' These comments invariably referred to an aspect of the organisation's structure or other colleagues. The data were coded independently by two raters on the 42 protocols we used in this part of the analysis (see Chapter 11) and a coefficient of +.83 was obtained between the two raters. Discrepancies were resolved by a third rater.

Sixty per cent of the direct-care staff in the study responded to this questionnaire, which we left with them during the course of the field work with a covering letter, instructions for its completion, and a stamp-

ed addressed envelope. They were asked to complete it at their own con-
venience and return it to us by mail. Each direct-care staff member was
assigned a code number which appeared on the questionnaire. We did
this because we hoped to use some of the data for individual level analyses.
Direct-care staff were assured of anonymity to the extent that no one
other than the research workers would be able to identify the questionnaire.
Some staff members who found the identifying code objectionable asked
to be allowed to remove it and, having done so, did return the questionnaires. This meant that for the purposes of some of the analyses, our
sample was further limited. The use of this code may well have deterred
other care staff from responding and in part account for the lower rate
of reply we obtained in some residences.

[In the institution from which we received the lowest response rate
to this questionnaire, the matter was taken up with the union (AFL-
CIO) when the members objected. The compromise referred to above
was then worked out, but prior to this meeting the union steward
involved had already instructed some members not to complete the
questionnaires. The Union Executive's compromise did not carry any
weight with those members. We were not really surprised by this, as
we learnt in the course of the field work and at some preliminary
discussions with union members that there had been a series of
'investigations' at this institution in the recent past by local and state
officials. In these 'investigations' anonymity had been promised. The
promise had apparently been broken. Research workers, trying to
ensure that their own professional standards are adhered to, are unlikely to meet a sympathetic response in such situations. In fact only
a great deal of preliminary discussion with union executive members,
who accompanied us to each building meeting where our purposes and
timetable were explained to staff, and strict adherence to our professional code of ethics made field work in these settings a possibility.]

The range in response rates across the residences was from 33 per cent
to 93 per cent. In two buildings we got only a single response and we
therefore excluded these buildings from the part of our analysis concerning the direct-care staff's perceptions of the organisation's structure.
Needless to say we would have liked a more uniformly high response
rate and are aware of the limitations of these data in some instances.
However, we were able from the personnel records to check on the representativeness of our respondent group in terms of their age, sex, training and length of service. We found that our sample did not differ sig-

nificantly on these counts from their non-responding colleagues, suggesting that the data base is reasonably representative. Since we used these
data as 'attitudinal' and 'perceptual' measures, we were not concerned
to establish the face validity of the responses and limited resources did
not permit us to effect tests of reliability over time. The data derived
from these questionnaires, with all the reservations these methodological
limitations imply, are presented and discussed in Chapter 11.

[We did not originally conceive of our attendant questionnaire data
as a measure of attendant staff perspective/attitudes. We initially
thought that since the questions referred to matters of 'fact', we
would obtain some consensus among members of a residence staff in
the characterisation of their work situations. However, the results
from the questionnaires simply did not support this interpretation.
There was often considerable disagreement among staff in a building
regarding such 'factual' matters as whether they had written work
rules, for example. Only in half of the residences did more than 75
per cent of the respondents agree regarding this 'fact'. Thus we must
regard the data as more appropriately representing staff attitudes
about these matters.]

We collected data on centralisation, communication and morale from
the building heads, in this instance using an interview. It was somewhat
difficult to determine who the building head was. A shift system operated so that there was usually both a morning and an afternoon charge
attendant. In some instances, there was more than one charge attendant
on each shift. We tried to interview only the charge attendant on the
morning shift, but where there was more than one such person we interviewed both of them. In one building there was no charge attendant at
all, so we interviewed the most senior attendant.

[At institutions A and B, in seven and two of the residences respectively, there were people described as 'matrons' in daily charge of the
buildings. This civil service grade was one grade higher than that of
charge attendant. It was being phased out, but in these instances we
perforce had to interview the 'matrons in charge'.]

We developed an index of centralisation from the building supervisor's responses to eleven questions about involvement in decisions
relating (a) to the residents, and (b) to the allocation and deployment
of subordinates. Responses to questions relating to these two areas cor-

related significantly ($r = +.56$), and we thus thought it reasonable to combine them into one index. Responses to each question were scored on a four-point scale—from no involvement to total authority. We obtained a building score by summing these item scores. Scores on this index ranged from 0 to 33; the lower score indicating a situation where all of the items were ones in which the building heads had total authority to make decisions. The higher score corresponded to a centralised situation, in which the building heads were never involved in decision making in any area, decisions always being made by a superior.

From responses to questions about the frequency of contact with representatives of eight different professional groups (all of whom in principle could have had reason to communicate with the building heads about the residents) we developed an index of communication with professionals. We gave a weight of four where meetings occurred daily, three for weekly meetings, two for monthly meetings and one where meetings between building heads and these professionals occurred rarely or never. Since eight professional groups were involved, the possible range of scores on this summary index is from 8 to 32, the lower score representing the least communication with professionals. Communication with unit directors and with members of other shifts was measured by two indices parallel to those described above.

The building supervisor interviews also provided us with data on their age, sex, training and length of service, as well as the overall staffing complement in the building. Indices of morale, in terms of attitudes to colleagues and to the work situation, were collected and analysed in the way described for direct-care staff. We did not collect data on formalisation at this level of the organisation, by oversight rather than design.

We regard the data collected from these interviews on centralisation, communication and morale as measures of the building heads' perceptions of these dimensions of organisational structure. As no independent validation of these responses was carried out we think it more appropriate to describe the data in these terms rather than as direct measures of organisational structure.

Data on the specialisation of task allocation between building heads and subordinate direct-care workers were obtained by observation using a time sampling technique. All staff on duty were observed for a period of two hours from the start of the day shift, i.e. 6.30 or 7 a.m., and again for two hours from the start of the evening meal. The observations were organised as follows. The building head was observed first, then a member of the direct-care staff group, each member of staff being observed for a total of three minutes, divided into one-minute intervals.

In each of these intervals, the staff member was observed for 30 seconds, followed by 30 seconds for recording. Where more than one representative of each group was on duty, the order in which the representatives were observed was determined from a prearranged random sequence established as soon as it was known who was to be on duty during the observation period. During these periods, we observed the activities of the staff and their interaction with the residents. Staff activities were classified into five general categories: administrative, domestic, supervisory, physical care, and social care of the residents. Each category of activities was defined by reference to a checklist of activities. A brief description of the activity was recorded, as well as the category code, so that codings could be checked in the research office. A sixth category, miscellaneous, was used for activities not subsumed under the other five categories.

The observations were carried out by five observers and reliability checks were made frequently. From a total sample of 593 observation periods in seven different settings, the overall coefficient of concordance for activity codes was .85. It was .89 for domestic activity, .91 for administration, .79 for supervisory activities, .90 for physical care, .66 for social care, and .93 for the occurrence of interaction between staff and residents. From these observations we developed an index of task specialisation, by establishing the differences between the proportion of time allocated by the building heads and the direct-care staff to each of the five activity types. These five differences were then summed to produce an overall specialisation index, giving a single score for each building. The higher the score, the greater the role specialisation in the building between the two status groups of staff. These findings are described in Chapter 12.

Gaining Entry

To obtain the data we have referred to in this and the preceding chapter we first approached the Assistant Commissioner of Mental Retardation in the Commonwealth's Department of Mental Health. He gave consent for the study to be undertaken in Institution A. By the time we were ready to work in two more state institutions, a new Assistant Commissioner had been appointed. This was a civil service post, ostensibly with tenure, but *de facto* a political appointment. The new incumbent refused permission for the study to continue until a meeting had been arranged at which we were to explain our project to all the regional directors of mental retardation. We met with these personnel from all parts of the state, and they directed us to approach the superintendents of the institutions to obtain their permission to carry out the work. We had of course done this in Institution A, and followed, in these two other settings, the procedures we had adopted there.

After discussing with the superintendent our research objectives and describing our data-gathering procedures, we met with union officials to whom the same statements were made. We then met with the unit directors and department heads, explaining our purposes and the extent to which we should need to work with them. We then arranged with the unit directors and union officials to attend as many meetings as necessary to ensure that all building staff were informed of the nature of the research and to answer any questions people might have. After these meetings, timetables were established for the research staff to carry out data collection in each setting and arrangements were made for interviews with the superintendents, unit directors, and department heads. The research workers informed the building heads of the detailed timetable for the week or ten days they would be spending in their building, and negotiated times for interviews with them and their subordinates.

A great deal of effort went into establishing these contacts, and all of it seems to have been necessary. The institutions had never had a good press and many staff were understandably suspicious of our work. We think that what at times seemed to us the interminable repetition of our purpose and methods was essential. We also think that our policy of showing staff what we were recording during observations when and if they asked to see the material was helpful in allaying anxieties. We know that without the help of the unions, as well as the superintendents and unit directors, we could not have carried out the data collection, not only in terms of obtaining interviews with them, but more importantly in terms of data collection in the residences. We could not have collected data at the building level, needless to say, without the forbearance of the staff who worked there, nor without the tolerance of the residents for our intrusions into what, after all is said and done, were their homes.

Summary

In sum, data were collected on 1,075 residents in 21 residences. Twenty building heads were interviewed, and 125 direct-care staff returned questionnaires to us.

[In the other residence where no charge attendant or matron worked, the interview was held with the most senior attendant.]

All three superintendents were interviewed, as were unit directors of the nine units in which the residences studied were incorporated. The heads of the departments of medicine, nursing, social work, and psychology were also interviewed, as were the stewards and treasurers of each institution. Basic demographic data on all these groups are presented in Part 3. The chart below summarises the data we collected and the techniques we used. It also indicates in which appendices the instruments used for data collection can be found and the chapters in which the analyses of the material are described.

Areas Studied and Methods Used

AREAS OF INSTITUTIONAL LIFE	TECHNIQUES OF DATA COLLECTION
The Residents	
1. Daily living skills, academic skills, behaviour problems, age, sex, activities, clothing.	Questionnaire for each resident completed by direct-care staff. (See Appendix 1:1 and Chapters 5 and 10)
2. IQ.	Data abstracted from institutional records. (See Chapters 5 and 10)
Care Provided for the Residents	
1. Management of daily and other recurring events.	Interview with building head and observations. (See Appendix 1:2 and Chapter 8)
2. Speech used by residence staff to residents.	Time sampled observations of residence staff. (See Appendix 1:3 and Chapter 8)
3. Physical environment.	Physical environment inventory. (See Appendix 1:4 and Chapter 8)
4. Contact with the Community.	Interview with building head. (See Appendix 1:5 and Chapter 8)
Organisation and Attitudes of Residence Staff	
1. Direct-care staffs' morale, perceptions of organisational structure, age, sex, length of service and training.	Self-administered questionnaire. (See Appendix 1:6 and Chapter 11)
2. Building heads' morale, perceptions of organisational structure, residence staffing, age, sex, length of service and training.	Interview with building heads. (See Appendix 1:7 and Chapter 12)
3. Specialisation of role.	Observation using time sampling of building heads and direct-care staff. (See Appendix 1:8 and Chapter 12)
Unit Structure	
1. Unit organisation and staffing.	Interview with unit director. (See Appendix 1:9 and Chapter 13)
2. Characteristics of unit directors: age, sex, training, length of service.	Interview with unit director. (See Appendix 1:9 and Chapter 13)
Departmental Organisation	
1. Organisation of departments and relation to units.	Interview with departmental heads. (See Appendix 1:10 and Chapter 13)

Institutional Organisation and Goals

1. Overall structure and goals of the institutions.

Interview with Chief Executive. (See Appendix 1:11 and Chapter 13)

Part Three

CHARACTERISTICS OF THE RESIDENTS AND RESOURCES

5 THE RESIDENTS

Administrators may develop policy about residential services and implement it, legislators determine appropriations, politicians make pious speeches, and planners write documents. But at one level it is arguable that it is the residents of the places who first determine the tasks to be carried out. Thus we begin our description with them.

Our study took place in three settings, in which lived a total of 3,240 mentally retarded people. For reasons already described, we focused on the lives of 1,075 of them.

Even a casual visitor to several residences in these institutions is quickly struck by their differences. In one residence, adolescents and young men, fashionably dressed, chat politely and appropriately with one another and the visitor about sports, politics, or the weather. Next door a group of elderly ladies, incessantly rocking, shower the visitor with bizarre greetings, inarticulate murmurings, mutterings, and angry gestures.

In the 21 buildings we studied, there were males and females ranging in average age from 22 to 56, and in average IQ from 12.5 to 59.1. In Table 5.1 we present the age, sex, and IQ distribution for all the residents, and also give the numbers of residents who were living in each of the buildings.

In some of the buildings we often found ourselves engaged in long conversations with the residents, whilst in others we found few people who could speak. In some residences we studied, newspapers were part of life for some, and painting in oils for others. Yet in another residence such activities were no part of any resident's life. There were buildings in which the residents seemed to spend their entire day aimlessly walking up and down or sitting staring from wooden benches. Yet all of these were residents, it must be remembered, of the same institutions. Clearly there are marked differences between the buildings in terms of the functional levels of their residents, and to a lesser extent in terms of their ages. We quickly learnt that these differences reflected a deliberate institutional policy, the policy of functional unitisation which we have referred to in Chapter 2. The residents in all three institutions were administratively grouped into what were described as functional units. This term was used to describe the purpose of the units. For the adult populations with which we were concerned, various labels had been

Table 5.1: Age, Sex, Number and IQ of Residents

Unit	Building	Age Mean	SD	Sex	Size	IQ Mean	Standard Deviation
1. Vocational	1	21.9	3.1	F	31	51.3	11.1
Unit I	2	45.1	13.1	M	92	41.8	15.9
	3	30.4	9.5	F	50	53.3	10.5
2. Vocational	4	33.1	8.1	F	92	37.4	16.2
Unit II	5	27.6	8.9	M	26	56.2	11.3
	6	26.8	10.2	M	59	28.0	16.6
	7	32.3	10.4	M	27	54.2	11.3
	8	44.6	12.3	F	51	43.7	11.4
3. Training	9	25.4	7.5	M	35	19.1	12.9
Unit	10	43.4	12.2	M	39	14.9	8.1
4. Training	11	37.6	10.8	F	67	15.2	8.0
Unit	12	30.6	9.4	F	30	26.5	12.6
—	13	16.1	2.5	F	33	35.9	10.6
5. Old Adult Unit	14	58.8	7.4	M & F	25	44.7	14.8
6. Young Adult	15	32.5	5.9	M	70	33.3	13.9
Unit	16	31.1	7.3	F	82	42.2	16.1
7. Behaviour Unit	17	28.9	7.3	M	59	12.5	3.2
8. Vocational Rehabilitation	18	36.8	11.9	F	21	59.1	14.1
Unit	19	35.0	12.3	M	35	52.0	13.7
9. Comprehensive	20	32.8	10.4	M & F	75	22.5	13.9
Care Unit	21	47.2	12.6	F	76	46.1	16.11

assigned to these groupings. In Institution A, Units 1 and 2 were called 'vocational units', and Units 3 and 4 were called 'training units'. In Unit 1 were Buildings 1, 2 and 3, and in Unit 2 were Buildings 4 to 8. Units 3 and 4 subsumed Buildings 9 and 10, and 11 and 12 respectively. In Institution B, two of the three units we worked in were described as 'Old Adult' and 'Young Adult', these being Units 5 and 6. In the former was Building 14 and in the latter Buildings 15 and 16. The third unit there was called the 'Behaviour Unit' and we studied one building in this, namely Building 17.

In Institution C we worked in two units which were called the Vocational Rehabilitation Unit (Unit 8) and the Adult Comprehensive Care Unit, which we call Unit 9. Buildings 18 and 19 were in the former unit and 20 and 21 were in the latter.

[Building 13 in Table 5.1 was not, as far as we could determine, assigned to a unit. It has been included in some of the analyses, where the significance of unit membership is of no consequence for the analyses involved.]

In practice, this 'functional' grouping of residents meant that units would have populations which differentiated them, one from another, in terms of ability level and age, as well as the 'purposes' for which they existed. It meant not only that the goals of the staff would be different for different residents, but that by and large less able residents would be housed separately from more able residents. Since we were focusing our attention on an adult group of residents, the issues of age segregation were obviously less marked than if we had looked at a children's unit and an adult one. The unit plan had not been completely rationalised, for although there were differences between the units on these counts, their populations in some cases varied widely in terms of both the age and ability of the residents, and in consequence we found residents in different units who were similar to each other on either or both of these characteristics. For example, the residents in Unit 1 were roughly similar in level of handicap (largely moderately retarded), but they ranged quite considerably in terms of their age, from people in their early twenties to people in their 50s. By way of contrast, Unit 2 had a wide range in the functional ability of its residents, some of whom were severely retarded, others moderately so. As a group their ages varied somewhat less than the residents in Unit 1, however. (Unit 2, mean age: 37.2, standard deviation 9.9; Unit 1, mean age 36.7, standard deviation 11.0.) The residents in Units 3 and 4 are much more comparable in terms of their average IQ and clearly much less able than residents in Units 1 and 2. Unit 9, like Unit 2, had a marked range in the functional ability of its residents, though its population was primarily middle-aged adults.

Six of the units had both male and female members, two had only males, and one females only. Two of the institutions actually went so far as permitting males and females to share the same building. In one case the average IQ of the group involved was 44.7, and in the other it was 22.5. What administrative nostrom generated these variations still remains a mystery to us.

In essence, while homogenisation in terms of age and IQ of the population was a clear characteristic of these institutions, it was somewhat more visible at building than at unit level. Some unit directors, however, like their building staffs, were coming to know the meaning of this administrative concept, at least in terms of its 'functional' implications. We were able to watch, in Institution C, as the process of homogenising the units was further implemented. There, the few remaining profoundly and severely retarded residents still housed with more able souls were being shipped into a three-storey building where they would be with others like themselves. The experience of watching 75 severely handicapped people being herded into one place, the staff's despair, and the superb irony of accommodating the most handicapped on the top floor, would have led us to question the wisdom of such 'functional' grouping, even if our research findings had not pointed to some danger-ous consequences (see Part Five). Denuded men crowded into a top-floor porch, the sounds of heads banging on polished lino floors, the endless struggling to find the key, observation schedules in hand, and the fear engendered in us by the apprehension of the ward staff about the behaviour of their charges confronted with 'strangers'—all these are not easily forgotten, nor are they represented well by tables of numbers.

Not all the institutions have gone so far in rationalising their plan 'functionally' to group the residents, but Institution C clearly pointed the direction in which they were all ostensibly moving. In at least two of the three institutions we worked in, such 'functional unitisation' still had some way to go. However, there were clear differences in the character-istics of the populations housed in the residences. It is at this level, rather than at unit level, that we have primarily focussed our attention. In Chap-ter 8, we discuss how the attributes of the residents in each building defined the situation of work for the direct-care staff, and the implic-ations of these resident characteristics for the provision of care.

To summarise, then. In those residences of the institutions we chose to study, there were males and females ranging in average age from 22 to 56 and in average IQ from 12.5 to 59.1. The residents were accom-modated in 21 buildings, which varied in terms of the numbers of residents housed in them from one residence with 21 residents to one with 92.

6   THE STAFF AND THE PHYSICAL SETTING

For so varied a group of people, what resources were made available? Let us consider first the material fabric which surrounded their lives. We go into detail about the interior of the buildings which were 'home' for the over 1,000 residents in our studies in Chapter 8. Here let us paint what we can in the way of a picture of the community they inhabited – what we saw as we visited for the first time, what they saw day in and day out.

The Physical Plant

The first institution was sited in the middle of a suburban community and a bus infrequently went past the main gate. A ten-minute walk could bring one out to the local shopping centre, where buses went frequently to the nearby cities. From the entrance, and the perimeter of part of the grounds, the houses and gardens of suburbia could easily be seen. The other two institutions were more isolated. Institution B was distinctly rural, but the bus, we were told, made trips to the nearby city an occasional possibility. We never saw it, and a car seemed a necessity if an unwooded landscape was ever sought. In Institution C, a 20-minute walk down a long driveway brought one into the local town, a depressed, small industrial place which had little to offer its own citizens, let alone the inhabitants of the institution. In all three places grass and trees surrounded the residences but the paintwork on the buildings was so faded that the colour was indeterminate.

Institutions A and C were architecturally variable, at least in the size and age of their buildings. Most of the residences were constructed on some H-shaped master plan, devised in the late nineteenth or early twentieth century (indeed so ubiquitous was this plan that although the institutions were 100 miles apart, it was often difficult to know where one was). These were typically of two- or three-storey construction with 'day room', dining room, two or four large dormitories or 'wards', and a small room used by the staff known as 'the office'. There were rooms for storage, isolation, laundry and kitchen activities, and visitors. Some of the buildings were originally cottages for staff, and these were smaller, having bedrooms, a living room, and a kitchen. Other buildings were products of the 1950s and 1960s. These more recent additions did not add architectural prestige, however. The most recent was a three-storey building in which a T-shaped design had been used. The interior had tiled yellow walls with terrazzo floors, each dormitory being linked by an office, a nurses' observation station, with small rooms off a long corridor and stair wells that rang in the same way as those built 50 years previously. Institution B had the dubious distinction of providing some uniformity in architecture, in so far as the accommodation it provided for residents was concerned. Its buildings, constructed in the 1930s, were three-storey, barrack-like edifices. Each had dormitories, 'day rooms', dining rooms with kitchens, and a complement of 'service rooms'.

The 'administration building', where the superintendent and other senior administrators were housed, was always part of the landscape. Occasionally flowers could be seen growing outside these buildings. Also regular features of the landscape in these three places were a recreation centre, a school, a laundry, and a central supply store and kitchen. One of the institutions had a shop where residents could buy sweets and toiletries. This was the most isolated of the three total communities. In a limited sense they were all total, limited in that most of us would expect a total community to contain a far wider variety of facilities than any of these three did. They were all wooded and the grass was carefully tended. One had its own park and the other two their own woods. Coming from the 'outside' we could see all this, but we rarely saw residents looking at it too.

The Care Staff

Who works in these uninspiring buildings, sharing them with the residents for at least part of the day? Let us begin by describing the actual care staff: the staff 'on the wards' or 'in the buildings', to use the local patois, the attendants and charges or matrons, as they were labelled by the state civil service codes. We chose, as we have noted, to refer to these two groups as the direct-care staff and the building heads, or supervisors. We must begin by noting that there are few formal rewards attached to their position. The job is an extremely low-paying one (the starting salary when we were working was $117 per week for attendants) and the hours are often inconvenient. The three shifts, which are ubiquitous, are from 7.0 a.m. to 3.30 p.m., 3.0 p.m. till 11.30 p.m., and 11.0 p.m. to 7.30 a.m.

We found the direct-care staff at all three institutions to be predominantly young: 45.4 per cent at Institution B, 38.1 per cent at Institution C, and 73.2 per cent at Institution A were under the age of 30. Table 6.1 shows the age distribution of our sample of the staff working in the buildings at the three institutions.

Table 6.1: Age of Direct-Care Staff

| | | Institutions | | | | | | |
| | A | | B | | C | | Total | |
Age	No.	%	No.	%	No.	%	No.	%
21	5	6.1	1	4.5	2	9.5	8	6.4
21-30	55	67.1	9	40.9	6	28.6	70	56.0
31-40	3	3.7	2	9.1	3	14.3	8	6.4
41-50	5	6.1	3	13.6	5	23.8	13	10.4
51 +	13	15.9	7	31.8	5	23.8	25	20.0
NI	1	1.2	–	–	–	–	1	0.8
	82	100.0	22	100.0	21	100.0	125	100.0

It should be noted that these data, like those in Tables 6.2, 6.3 and 6.4, derive from our voluntary questionnaire; however, our respondents did not differ significantly in these characteristics from those who did not respond. Sixty per cent of the direct-care staff in 20 of the 21 buildings studied filled out the questionnaire, comprising the 125 members in our sample.

The second largest age group was over 51 (20 per cent of the total staff in the three institutions). This is not surprising when we consider the labour force available to the three institutions.

Institution A, being located within a large metropolitan area with many colleges and universities, has almost three quarters of its direct-care staff under the age of 30. This is no doubt attributable to the availability of students, who are at an interim time in their careers. Many of the staff in our study indicated that they were working as attendants while they were working out what to do with their lives. The large number of staff over 51 in Institutions B and C expresses a different economic reality; Institution B, which has the highest percentage of staff in this age group (31.8), is located in a rural part of the state where there is little in the way of local industry or alternative employment.

Table 6.2 shows the staff of the three institutions with regard to sex. Of the total 125 respondent staff, 58.4 per cent are females, and this figure is close to those for two of the institutions, A and C, B having somewhat fewer female and more male staff members. This figure is **striking when** we consider that considerably less than half of the labour

Table 6.2: Sex of Direct-Care Staff

| | Institutions | | | | | | Total | |
| | A | | B | | C | | | |
	No.	%	No.	%	No.	%	No.	%
Male	32	39.0	12	54.5	7	33.3	51	40.8
Female	50	61.0	9	40.9	14	66.7	73	58.4
NI	–	–	1	4.5	–	–	1	0.8
	82	100.0	22	100.0	21	100.0	125	100.0

force is comprised of women. From informal conversations and from responses to the questionnaire, we can infer that many of these female staff members are providing second incomes for their families. Consistent with this, we observed a relationship between sex and marital status in the sample: 53 per cent of the female staff reported their status as 'married' on our questionnaire, as compared with only 35 per cent of the male staff. We would guess that this differential expresses an economic fact: these relatively low-paying direct-care positions are financially inadequate as the primary income for many families.

With regard to training, perhaps our most outstanding finding was that there was little among the staff. Although we would expect that some of the students would have had some psychology or special education courses in college, only 16.8 per cent of the staff had degrees in these or related fields. As can be seen from Table 6.3, a full 69.6 per cent had no formal training at all.

The figures are similar for in-service training as well: 60 per cent of all staff in our sample had not attended in-service training.

We also asked on our questionnaire about staff residence, and found that only eleven per cent over all resided on the grounds of the institutions, in the small staff residence halls available. Thus, for the overwhelming majority of staff, these 'total institutions' were only a part of daily life.

When we look at how long staff members have been at their jobs, we find a wide variety of length of service, ranging from under three months to over 25 years. More than half (61.6 per cent) have been at their job at least one year, but only 44 per cent have remained on the job over two years. It seems clear that a relatively high level of staff turnover is endemic to these residential facilities.

All these staff were deployed in specific buildings. Staffing ratios

Table 6.3: Formal Training of Direct-Care Staff

| | Institutions | | | | | | Total | |
| | A | | B | | C | | | |
	No.	%	No.	%	No.	%	No.	%
Degree in Special Education	2	2.4	0	0.0	0	0.0	2	1.6
Degree in Rehabilitation	0	0.0	0	0.0	0	0.0	0	0.0
Degree in Psychology	9	11.0	1	4.5	0	0.0	10	8.0
Other Degree	7	8.5	1	4.5	1	4.8	9	7.2
Nursing training (RN, LPN, Diploma)	0	0.0	0	0.0	0	0.0	0	0.0
Other training	8	9.8	3	13.6	3	14.3	14	11.2
No training	56	68.3	15	68.2	16	76.2	87	69.6

were extraordinarily varied between the buildings, as Table 6.4 makes clear. Our average ratios are crude estimations based on staff available over one week of field work for the 7.0 a.m. to 3.30 p.m. shift and the 2.30 p.m. to 11.0 p.m. shift. Rarely were there more than two people on the 11.0 p.m. to 7.0 a.m. 'night' shift, and usually only one.

Chapters 10 and 11 will consider the implications for care of these patterns of variation between residences in the demographic features of staff.

The Building Heads

The building heads were paid little more than the attendants. In this group, those who were designated charge attendants started at a salary which

Table 6.4: Staffing Ratios in 21 Residences

Unit	Building No.	Ratio of staff to residents
1	1	1: 8.7
	2	1:11.9
	3	1:10.1
2	4	1:18.1
	5	1: 5.9
	6	1: 7.9
	7	1:10.7
	8	1:11.7
3	9	1: 4.7
	10	1: 4.9
4	11	1: 5.8
	12	1: 4.7
—	13	1: 8.3
5	14	1: 8.3
6	15	1:17.5
	16	1:18.5
7	17	1: 6.0
8	18	1: 5.5
	19	1: 5.0
9	20	1: 4.1
	21	1: 6.9

was ten dollars more than the starting salary of their attendant colleagues. The matrons in this group earnt only a few more dollars. Financially, then, this group had little to gain from their elevated status.

Of the 20 building heads we interviewed, twelve were female and eight were male. As a group they were clearly older than the direct-care staff: 19 of the 20 being over the age of forty. The same number had no formal training. In two cases, both in Institution A, the building heads had received some training before coming to the institution. One had a B.A. degree and the other was an LPN or Licensed Practical Nurse (roughly equivalent to an SEN in England). In-service training was equally uncommon in this group. Only one of them had received any such training during the year prior to our interviewing them. Fourteen of them had been in their current positions for more than five years, and six for a shorter time than this.

As a group, then, they were older than their subordinates and had been in their positions markedly longer. In terms of training they were essentially indistinguishable from the direct-care staff. Indeed, length of service, rather than any other demographic criterion, appears to have been the basis on which selection for promotion to the position of charge attendant or matron was made. The career structure ladder stopped at this point and further promotion would have entailed a lateral move and, in all probability, training. Thus, once an appointment to these positions had been obtained, it is not surprising that the staff stayed where they were. In Chapters 11 and 12 we shall have more to say about the role of the building heads, and the promotional system which produced them.

The Administrators

All three places had staff whose primary place of work did not involve a direct attachment to one of the buildings, or was not carried out in the buildings themselves. Each institution had a superintendent. In two of them, the superintendents were medically trained and had been in their posts for 28 and 7 years respectively. In the third institution the superintendent had a doctorate in education and had been at his post for 13 months. Each superintendent had at least one deputy and was administratively 'supported' by a steward and a treasurer, each of these having his own staff. In Chapter 13 we describe these administrators in more detail. All three places had engineering and power plant departments, food services, garage and grounds, maintenance, laundry, post and telephone services, and a central records and personnel department. These 'maintenance' services were not the only departments the members of which had little directly to do with the residents. (In many cases. unless residents actually worked 'in' these services, the staff there could go about their daily business and neither hear nor see any mentally handicapped person.) There were also what were called 'professional' departments. Each institution had its medical and nursing departments, an education department, a psychology department, and a social work service. Institution A was more richly endowed with special professional services than either B or C, perhaps because of its proximity to several universities. Physical therapy, speech and hearing therapy, and occupational therapy, as well as rehabilitation and vocational training, were amongst the services present at Institution A.

What did this vast array of skilled professional talent mean if one lived and/or worked in a building? The answers to that question were remarkably varied, depending on the building involved.

Table 6.5: Professional Services Assigned to Units

Unit	MD	Nurse	Psych.	Teachers	R.	SW	OT	PT	Rehab.	Total number services assigned
1	X	X	X	—	X	X	—	—	—	5
2	X	X	X	—	—	X	—	—	—	4
3	X	X	—	—	X	—	—	—	—	3
4	X	X	X	—	—	—	—	—	—	3
5	X	X	—	—	—	—	—	—	—	2
6	X	X	X	—	—	X	—	—	—	4
7	X	X	X	X	—	X	X	X	X	8
8	X	X	X	—	—	X	—	—	—	4
9	X	X	X	X	—	X	X	—	—	6

Note: MD   = Physician
      Nurse   = Nurse
      Psych.   = Psychologist
      Teachers = Teachers
      R.   = Recreational specialists
      SW   = Social workers
      OT   = Occupational therapists
      PT   = Physical therapists
      Rehab.   = Rehabilitation specialists

Table 6.5 makes it clear that not all units and therefore buildings in them were in receipt of the range of professional services theoretically available in the institution's organisational chart. Neither size of unit nor functional level of the residents has any effect on the numbers of professionals assigned to work in a unit.

The richness of resources, in terms of years of acquired professional training or cost to the taxpayer, means little if the service such people can provide is seen rarely by those people for whom it is intended. The implications of professional support for the care of the handicapped residents are discussed in Chapters 12 and 13.

Into this set of tangled organisational relationships, exacerbated as they already were by differences in length of tenure and professional and other allegiances, the unit directors had been drafted to spearhead the revolution from custodial to humane care. They were essentially middle-line managers with functions and authority, as we shall later

describe, not very clearly defined. They were as diverse in their characteristics as were the residents for whom they were responsible. Six of the
nine we studied were male, eight were married, and seven of them lived
outside the institution. One was a nurse. Of the others, six had masters
degrees, two in rehabilitation, one in psychology, one in social work,
one in education and one in sociology. The other two had completed
first degrees, one in sociology and one in theology.

Only one third had been in their present position for more than two
years. Four of the unit directors had in fact been in the post for less
than one year. Two thirds of them were under the age of 30. Their
relative youth, both chronologically and in terms of their service within
the institution, made them novices. Yet they were charged with the
sometimes herculean job of co-ordinating services and programmes for
the residents. Their job specifications stated that they would 'direct the
unit team' and supervise all personnel assigned to a 'functional unit'.
Perhaps symbolic of the difficulties in the way of this charge, only three
of the unit directors had offices in a building which was part of their
unit; two were located in the 'administration building', and four of
them had no offices at all! In Chapters 12 and 13, we consider how
these new managers were coping with the difficult role assigned to
them, and their impact on the lives of the residents involved.

The total number of staff working in these places was surprisingly
hard to determine. The superintendents did not know the names of the
department heads (in one case the superintendent did not know how
many departments there were), and endless games were played with the
civil service allocation of 'blocks', as the posts for all staff were called.
Attendants (a lower civil service grade) were hired in lieu of nurses,
painters in lieu of secretaries, and so on. Endless inter-departmental
wars were fought over the way in which blocks were to be used. From
varied sources, we estimate that at the time of the study, the personnel
supporting and serving all of the residents in the three institutions
numbered about 3,000. The cost to the taxpayer per year for these
services was around 38 million dollars. No small enterprise and no small
community of souls. What the ministrations of these providers meant
for the residents' care we begin to describe in Chapter 8.

7 SOME SKETCHES FROM INSTITUTIONAL LIFE

We close this part of the book by moving from the numbers we have presented to some of the images we recall. None of us believe that numbers alone can ever provide a sense of the smells, sights and sounds, or the texture of life where large groups of human beings are gathered together living out their lives. For some, the institution bounded their lives like an extraordinary island, while others moved in and out of it on a rhythmic tide of 'shifts': those 'cared for' and the 'carers'. The numbers we have presented in their neat rows and columns tidy up the kaleidoscope of this daily life, of these communities of people. They help us see them clearly in one sense, just because of this tidying up. But words and images are needed to convey the variegated smells, sights and sounds, the people, and the places they lived and worked in, endlessly presented to each other as well as to us. In our fieldwork there was time to talk and work outside the structure imposed on us by stop watches and interview schedules. We all found we needed to walk between the buildings, to the astonishment of the staff, who invariably drove. Those walks in some little way helped us to deal with the vast array of stimuli that came through our protective research armour and clearly defined non-participant roles. Some of these experiences we recall here.

Eighty-year-old A who called us over one warm summer evening to share part of his birthday cake, his slippered feet partly shrouded by his low-hanging grey worn trousers. 'The Matron', who showed us with pride the shining brass plate in the floor polished every day by her 'girls'.

The pride with which the new pink-tiled showers, each with shower curtains, were shown to us, and the seriousness with which the propriety of our watching the young ladies shower was discussed.

The piles of rubbish in the inner well of a three-storey building, and the rusting wire netting surrounding the porches which looked down into the well.

The smell of urine in a building for 'ladies' whom one could see in a 'day room' over the stable door.

The omnipresent argot of the institution: every residence had its 'day room', its 'ward' for sleeping, its 'office' for the staff.

A social argot too: residents and staff discussing others, the labels 'high grade' or 'low grade' so readily used, so clear in their implications.

The hustle and hard work of a young staff member, bent on applying behaviour modification principles—teaching some nearly toothless old men to brush their teeth for the first time in their lives.

A row of men in their twenties waiting on a bench in a room bare of curtains or other furniture, except for a table on which was equipment being used to teach them colour discrimination. The men sitting passively, their clothes soiled, their eyes listless. The air stale with the smell of urine. The bored young staff members, modifying as instructed.

Listening to a 25-year staff veteran talking about 'the good old days', when the residents weren't 'really' retarded and the building workers were 'really' boss.

Watching a 16-year-old summer staff worker 'supervise' a group of 50-year-old retarded men, out for their evening walk around the 'yard'. The grisled faces of the men gradually blurring in the twilight.

The extraordinary silence, loneliness, endlessness of the night shift worker's job as we watched him waken and line up dozing naked men at 5.30 a.m. for their morning toileting.

The interminable card games and TV watching at the employees' canteen; the younger 'hip' staff members sharing a smoke; the routine, comfortable joking of staff members in a residence for profoundly retarded.

The gloomy area at the entrance to the canteen, flag-stoned, where one machine dispensed packaged sandwiches, another one tea or coffee.

The swingers of the resident population; standing awkwardly like uncomfortable adolescents at the monthly institution-wide dance, men and women along opposite walls.

The heat in winter and summer of buildings with temperatures of 80° and 90° and higher.

The deafening crash of doors being slammed by a powerfully built, severely retarded man running through a building in a rage; the building staff alternately trying to restrain him, then staying out of his way.

The attendant who said 'it's her smile that makes it worth while'; a smile that when it finally came made us only think that oral hygiene was sadly lacking in this place.

Two elderly parents visiting their 40-year-old, retarded daughter: the hopeless resignation, tempered by love, in their lined faces.

A research building, curtains at its windows and carpets on its floors, brightly painted, overlooking the grilled uncurtained windows behind which was the 'yard' for profoundly retarded adolescent men.

Obviously the three institutions (what other word can we use?) were not all of a piece. Going into a building could sometimes be a pleasant

experience. Sometimes instead, all that has ever been written about
custodial bleak institutions was a living reality for the resident, for 24
hours a day, seven days a week, for the staff for the duration of their
duty, and for us for a week or ten days of our lives. Those who lived
there were varied in their appearance, ability, age and their sex, their
memories, their interests, and their activities. Those who 'worked' there
came from different backgrounds, professional groups, and economic
strata. What the latter did for the former, and some of the reasons why,
we hope to make clear in Parts Four and Five which follow.

Part Four

VARIATIONS IN CARE

8 FOUR DIMENSIONS OF CARE

In the United States Belknap (1956), Goffman (1961), Blatt & Kaplan (1966), Blatt (1969), and Nirje (1969), amongst others, have described bleak institutional environments. In Great Britain the Department of Health's Committee of Inquiry into Ely Hospital (1969), for example, showed that bad conditions occur in England too. All this work may well have had a salutary effect in drawing attention to the negative aspects of institutional life, but institutional care at least in the settings we studied is clearly not all of a piece. In all three institutions we studied, we found marked variations in care among the residences studied, and resident-oriented care clearly characterised the management of residents in some of the facilities.

We have described in Chapter 3 our reasons for looking at four areas of care provided for the residents, and the methods by which we attempted to measure these four aspects. Care in each of these areas was found to vary within Institution A, and within the units of this institution as well. Thus our view of the daily management of social situations, of the speech used by staff to residents, of the physical environment provided for them, and of their contact with the surrounding community, as dimensions best described as continua along which care can be seen to vary, was supported in our initial empirical analysis. The relative independence of these dimensions, described in Chapter 3, also provides support for our argument that the position of a residence on one of these dimensions will not necessarily indicate its position on another.

Morris (1969), McLain et al. (1975), and Holland (1973) have all presented evidence of variations in care, for at least one of the areas we studied, within institutions for the retarded. Morris in her discussion of physical provision noted that 'the specific environment of the patients may vary widely from ward to ward, so that any attempt to rate the hospital as a whole in terms of one criterion is likely to bear no more relationship to reality than the 2.4 child family of demographic calculations' (p. 87). McLain and his colleagues' finding, that a modified version of the scale developed by King et al. (1971), from which we derived the RRMP, differentiated not only between treatment programmes in a facility but also between the wards within these programmes, gives support to Morris's argument.

It will be recalled that we selected four residences in Institutions B and C, matching them as best as we were able with the buildings we had observed first in Institution A, i.e. selecting residences which were similar in terms of the ability levels of the residents and their age. When we compared the three institutions on all our measures of care, we found that there were no statistical differences between them. In consequence we have treated the 21 residences as if they were one population, and do not differentiate between them unless there is a particular reason for doing so. Essentially our analyses of the care in the residences in these two other places replicated our findings in Institution A. In all three places we found marked variation *within* the settings. It is important to recognise the existence of such variation and seek out reasons for it, if we are ever to move towards improving the kinds of care we provide. Identifying the factors associated with resident-oriented care provides a basis from which to move towards ensuring it for all residents. We now turn to a discussion of our attempts to do this. In Part Three, we begin with a description of our findings about care, and in Part Four we shall turn to an examination of some of the factors that might account for these differences.

The Management of Daily Events

The RRMP measures the extent to which the management of recurrent social events is resident- or institution-oriented. King *et al.* (1971) argued that the questions in the scale focused on four distinct qualities of staff/resident interaction: rigidity of routine, block treatment, social distance and depersonalisation. These qualities are described by Goffman (1961) as characteristic of the interaction between staff and inmates in total institutions. McCormick and his colleagues (1975), in a factor analysis of this scale, could not find distinctive factors along these proposed dimensions, however. We therefore present the total score on the abbreviated 28-item version of the scale we applied in our settings. It will be recalled that the range of possible scores on this scale was from 0 to 56; the lower the score, the more resident-centred the care characterised by it. The distribution of the scores for the residences is given in Table 8.1, along with the scores of the residences on each of the other measures of care.

It can be seen that the range of scores on the RRMP is very wide, from 2 to 43 points. The mean for the 21 residences was 22.95, the standard deviation 10.73. There were no significant differences between the buildings located at the three different institutions on this measure. In Institution A we examined the scores of the units on this measure of care. The means and standard deviations for the four units to which buildings belonged are given in Table 8.2.

Table 8.1: Scores on the Measures of Quality of Care

Unit	Building	RRMP	ISI	IPE	ICI
1	1	18	30	30	32
	2	22	19	55	45
	3	14	37	29	20
2	4	28	32	52	42
	5	9	23	38	25
	6	31	22	66	41
	7	2	45	47	13
	8	18	38	32	43
3	9	30	12	82	48
	10	31	18	69	45
4	11	32	10	73	48
	12	23	41	50	33
–	13	30	23	65	44
5	14	11	40.4	33	25
6	15	28	48.2	53	70
	16	17	26.4	64	82
7	17	43	2.6	78	59
8	18	8	62.8	35	21
	19	17	19.1	49	35
9	20	40	29.3	67	75
	21	30	29.2	44	76

Table 8.2: Unit RRMP Scores, Mean and Standard Deviations, Institution A

	Unit 1	Unit 2	Unit 3	Unit 4
Mean	18.0	17.6	30.5	27.5
Standard Deviation	4.0	12.3	0.7	6.4

With the exception of Unit 3, there is considerable variance within the units on this measure of the care provided. These scores do not suggest that the grouping of buildings into units had any systematic or substantial effect on the kind of care being provided for the residents. To test this formally, a one-way analysis of variance was conducted on the scores of the two lowest-ability residences in Units 1 and 2, and the two residences of Units 3 and 4. This approach seemed a reasonable matching procedure for testing unit effects, and produced a non-significant result ($F_{3;4}=3.37$). This suggests to us that it is factors characteristic of the residence, rather than the administrative unit of which the residence is a part, that are of primary importance in influencing the quality of care as it is measured by this scale.

Clearly there is a wide range of care practices in the management of getting up, bed and mealtimes; birthdays; personal clothing; and access to rooms in the residences—the kind of issue covered in the RRMP. We will try to convey the import of these scale scores in two ways. First, we compare our findings to those of other studies of this dimension of care; and secondly, we present some descriptions of daily life under varied care practices. We cannot directly compare the scores on the RRMP with those on the Child Management Scale used in the study by King *et al.* (1971), because a smaller number of items were used in the RRMP. However, since the scoring procedure and data collection methods were identical for all the 28 items used in both scales, we can get a broader perspective on what it means to live in Building 7 as compared with Building 17, or Building 18 as compared with Building 20, by comparing the percentage scores in this study with the percentage scores on the measure used by King *et al.* (1971). In that study, the hostels' (community residences') scores ranged from 3.33 per cent to 36.67 per cent of the total possible score, with a mean of 18.33 per cent. The hospitals ranged in their scores from 61.67 per cent to 75.0 per cent, with a mean of 71.67 per cent. The most institution-oriented of all the living units they studied were found in this group of hospital wards. The range of scores in the 21 buildings in our study expressed as a percentage of the total scale score was 3.57 per cent to 76.78 per cent, almost identical to the range of scores they found existed *across* these two types of residential setting. In fact, nine residences in our study (Buildings 1, 3, 5, 7, 8, 14, 16, 18 and 19) had scores within the range of scores they found characterised the hostels in their study. Only two of the residences in our study had scores as high as those in the hospital wards they studied, namely Buildings 17 and 20. Ten of the residences had scores which ranged from 39 per cent of the total possible score to 57 per cent, and fell between the hostels and the hospital wards in the English study. Clearly, within the settings we examined, there can be found management practices as measured by the RRMP which are very similar to those that characterise the hostels surveyed in England. However, there also exist in these same settings residences where care is as institution-oriented as it was in the hospital wards. What we have to remember is that King and his colleagues were studying entirely different types of settings. The scores we have presented as characteristic of the management practices in these residences are (*a*) scores found *within* one setting, and (*b*) scores of residences in settings which were all of the same type. These American institutions were most comparable in terms of overall size and administrative identity to the English hospitals.

The quality of daily life indicated by these scores can perhaps best be illustrated if we compare descriptions of two residences that are similar in terms of the functional ability of the residents who lived there, but vary in their RRMP scores. Building 7 had a score of two on the RRMP and Building 21 had a score of 30 on the same scale.

Building 7, a two-storey structure, accommodates 27 mildly and moderately retarded males. This building attained the lowest score on the Revised Resident Management Practices Scale. The residents here come and go freely. They have their own bedrooms and share a common living space. They eat in a cafeteria in another building, determine for themselves when they go there, and do so unaccompanied by staff members. They bathe individually in bathrooms which have doors they can lock. They have their own clothes and places in their bedrooms to keep these, in addition to many personal possessions which give their rooms a very individualised look. Staff and residents often sit down together to talk or play card games. In the evenings, snacks are made in a small kitchen in the building, the residents and staff sharing the chores. There is an easy, relaxed atmosphere in the small building, and the residents have a sense of pride about themselves and their home, which they express frequently to visitors. Building 21 also accommodates moderately retarded residents. Seventy-six women live there. These residents are accommodated in four wards. Each ward has a day room and a dormitory. Whilst the day rooms have cheerful curtains the armchairs tend to be arranged in lines around the perimeter of the rooms. The dormitories are large and groups of chests used by individual residents are used to divide up the space. Meals are eaten in the dining room in the basement and everyone eats together at the same time. A bell rings, and residents are told to go downstairs. The tables are bare of utensils. These are collected at the cafeteria-style counter. Staff supervise the mealtime and pour out drinks for the residents. The staff are friendly but spend little time with the residents, who in the evenings are invariably watching television or rocking in their chairs.

For a few residents bathing is an individualised affair, but it is done in bathrooms where no privacy is possible. For the rest, it means lining up a few at a time to be showered down by other residents or staff. Leaving the building, even to sit outside, requires that there is a member of staff free to go with the resident in most cases. Residents are restricted, too, from using several of the rooms in the building which are considered staff rooms or offices. Despite efforts made by the staff to brighten up the building with pictures, curtains and even sofas, it is an uninviting and restrictive kind of environment. Unlike their counterparts in Building 7 these residents do not seem to take pleasure in showing visitors around their home.

The Speech Used by Staff to Residents

When we look at the scores on the ISI shown in Table 8.1 we see again that residences varied markedly. It will be recalled that this index is a measure of the frequency of occurrence of informative speech used by staff when residents were present, higher scores thus indicating a greater average percentage of informative remarks by staff. Thus the possible range of scores on this measure was from zero per cent to 100 per cent. The observed range in Institution A was from 10 to 45 per cent, with a mean 26.9 per cent, and a standard deviation of 11.1 per cent. In Table 8.3 we give the unit mean and standard deviation scores on this measure.

Table 8.3: Unit ISI Scores, Means and Standard Deviation, Institution A

	Unit 1	Unit 2	Unit 3	Unit 4
Mean	28.7	32.0	15.0	25.5
Standard Deviation	9.1	9.8	4.2	21.9

Again, membership in a unit seems to have no significant effect, as tested by a one-way analysis of variance for the eight matched buildings in Units 1-4 ($F_{3:4} = 0.38$). The variance on this measure was even greater in Institution B, from 2.0 per cent to 48.2 per cent. At Institution C, the range was from 19.19 per cent to 62.8 per cent. The means and standard deviation scores for the buildings selected at these two other institutions were, respectively, mean 29.4, SD 20.0; and mean 35.1, SD 19.1. The range for all 21 buildings on this measure was from 2.6 per cent to 62.8

per cent (mean = 28.9, SD = 14.1), as shown in Table 8.1.

It is obvious from these data that the residences do differ in the extent to which residents are spoken to informatively. In part, these differences depended on the likelihood of staff speaking at all. In several buildings we observed, the frequency of ten-second observation periods with at least one staff remark to the residents approached 90 per cent. On the other hand, in Building 17, which cared for profoundly retarded men, staff spoke to residents in less than one third of all observations. Almost all of these remarks (86 per cent) involved orders to the residents of one sort or another. Residents in this building would rarely hear chatty remarks about last night's TV shows or yesterday's shopping trip, or be asked their opinion about someone's new outfit—the type of inter-action characterising a number of other residences. Life in Building 17 was sterile and controlling in this respect at least. Normal conversational interchange, in which the listener replies to the speaker, was almost com-pletely lacking here—only one remark by staff in fifty received a reply. We should note here that our measure of informative speech was strongly correlated with the likelihood of resident reply ($r = .76$, $p < .01$).

In contrast, consider Building 10, which also housed profoundly re-tarded men. Here speech to residents was twice as likely over all, and informative remarks about seven times as common as in Building 17. Controlling remarks were only half as frequent here as in Building 17, and residents were more than ten times as likely to reply to the staff. Building 10 was by no means the best of all possible worlds, but there were many periods of real staff/resident conversation, some-times about serious topics. There was, indeed, something uniquely human about this type of talk, and its absence did seem to impoverish the res-idents' lives.

Some types of interaction are likely to promote learning. Tizard's work (1972) suggested that what we have called informative speech could promote development in the language comprehension and expres-sion of the residents. She found in her study that children's verbal skills were greater in the nurseries where staff used more 'informative' language. She was able to assess the children's linguistic skills through careful testing. We were not, but we have some limited evidence which suggests that in the contexts in which we worked, informative speech also pro-motes language development. We think that the use of such speech by staff is not just pleasanter or more interesting, but is also likely to promote skills in the residents who hear it.

In our collection of data about the residents' skills we asked two questions which related to their language comprehension and expression abilities. The staff were asked to rate each resident's ability on the follow-ing two scales: (*a*) comprehension: 1 = understands complex commands (two or more actions), 2 = understands simple commands only, 3 = under-stands one or two word action commands only, 4 = understands own name only, and 5 = no comprehension of language; (*b*) language expres-sion: 1 = speaks in complete sentences, 2 = speaks in phrases only, 3 = uses phrases and single words, 4 = uses single words only, and 5 = no recognisable speech. Inter-rater reliability for two staff members rating the same resident on the first was .84, and .70 on the second.

To assess the relationship between the amount of informative speech used and the residents' language performance, we averaged these indiv-idual ratings of comprehension and expression to generate indices for the residences. Having done this we found that in buildings where the average IQ of the residents was in the moderate to mild range, both the measures of comprehension and expression were invariably close to 'perfect' scores of 1.00. Because of this 'ceiling' effect on the measures, we decided to assess the association between resident speech abilities and the ISI only in the ten buildings with average resident IQ in the severe or profound range.

Using Spearman's rank correlation coefficient (because of the ordinal nature of the language skill measures), we found a significant positive correlation between the residents' language comprehension scores and the amount of informative speech used by the staff in the residence. This relationship between comprehension and the ISI was stronger than the correlation between comprehension and average resident IQ, which was not significant. We found a similar association between the residents' expressive scores and scores on the ISI but, in this instance, average res-ident IQ is more strongly associated with the expression scores than is the ISI (see Table 8.4).

Table 8.4: Indices of the Quality of Care and Resident Speech Abilities

	Correlations with average resident comprehension	Correlations with average resident expression
1. RRMP	-.79*	-.79*
2. ISI	+.60*	+.75*
3. Average Building IQ	+.54	+.87*

*p .05, one-tailed

Clearly these data can be no more than suggestive. First, they do not represent independent test data on the residents, but simply staff assessments of their abilities. Secondly, we are well aware that only a carefully designed longitudinal study could properly assess the impact of varying care practices on the residents' development. Nevertheless these data are consistent with the expectation that more informative speech used by staff to residents will have a beneficial effect on the residents' language development. Blindert (1975) observed the infrequent occurrence of verbal interaction between staff and residents in a children's ward in a facility for the mentally retarded. Most interaction there, when it occurred, was what we have called controlling, consisting of commands to do this or not to do that. He argued that if learning by the residents is to occur, staff will have to be trained to increase the frequency of their interactions which could promote such learning. We agree with this statement, and would suggest that more time spent by teaching staff in speaking informatively to residents might be one strategy for promoting certain aspects of language learning.

[Interestingly we found, when we examined the relationship between scores on the RRMP and these two measures of the residents language abilities, that exactly the same pattern of associations occurred as with the ISI and these two indices of resident language. This suggests to us that resident-oriented care in both these areas of the residents' lives will have positive effects on the residents' development. We clearly need a controlled longitudinal study to validate this assertion, but we should be willing to bet on the outcome of such a study.]

The Physical Environment

Scores on the IPE could range from zero to 88, the lower score representing maximum availability of the physical amenities included in the index. As can be seen in Table 8.1, the range of scores on this index was also very wide at Institution A, from 29 to 82 (mean 59.92, standard deviation 17.39). The means and standard deviations for the four units at Institution A are given in Table 8.5.

Table 8.5: Unit IPE Scores, Mean and Standard Deviation, Institution A

	Unit 1	Unit 2	Unit 3	Unit 4
Mean	38.0	47.0	75.5	61.5
Standard Deviation	14.7	13.2	9.2	16.3

A one-way analysis of variance for the usual eight comparison buildings at Institution A showed that membership in a unit had no effect on
the scores obtained on this measure as well ($F_3.4 = 1.93$, ns). At Institutions B and C we found ranges of scores on this measure from 33 to 78
and 35 to 67, respectively. The range for the 21 buildings there was 29
to 82 (mean = 52.9, standard deviation 16.4). We can more readily
understand the significance of these scores if we look first at the distribution of the amenities it describes across the 21 settings and then compare the situation in the highest and lowest scoring residence.

Seven of the items in the measure related to the provision of furniture
and furnishings in the day rooms or living rooms of the residences. All
but two of the residences had televisions available for the residents in
these rooms, but in over 80 per cent of the residences ten or more residents had to view the same set. There was only one building in which
one set was available for every five of the residents. Morris (1969), in
her survey of the physical environment provided in hospital wards in
England, noted that 89 per cent of the patients in the survey lived in
wards where a television was available. This was true for 93 per cent of
the residents in our study but the calculation of the availability of this
amenity as a ratio makes it clear that for the majority of the residents
the use of this amenity could rarely be a small group or individual activity. Armchairs and settees in which the residents could sit and relax,
whether to watch television or engage in any other pastime, were not
common in the majority of the residences. In 63 per cent of the residences there was less than one armchair for every two residents and one
building had none at all. Three buildings had no settees and in over three
quarters of the buildings a settee was only available to be shared between
a minimum of six residents. Occasional tables on which to play games
or sew, for example, were equally rare. One building had none and in
57 per cent of the residences this item was one which had to be shared
between a minimum of five residents. Although three fifths of these
living rooms had curtains or shades on the windows which brightened
the atmosphere a little the rooms for many residents were not comfortable places to sit and relax.

The furniture and furnishings in the bedrooms were also variable in
their distribution. Perhaps the most striking feature of these was the
number of residents who had to sleep in the same room. In only two
of the 21 buildings were residents sleeping in rooms of their own or
ones which they shared with only one other person. In the remaining
residences, a minimum of ten residents slept in the same room, more
accurately called a dormitory than a bedroom. In these rooms in six

buildings every resident had his or her own bedside locker and in seven buildings there was a wardrobe for every resident in which personal belongings could be kept. In a third of the buildings however there were no lockers at all, and in over half of them no wardrobe at all, either. Just over half of the residences had beds in the dormitories with drawers in them in which a limited number of personal possessions could be stored. Morris found that 43.3 per cent of the patients in her survey had exclusive use of a bedside locker and 24.7 per cent shared them. By comparison the situation in these 21 residences was considerably poorer, for only 14.6 per cent had use of one which they shared with one other person. An attempt to individualise the beds by providing different coloured bedspreads in each dormitory was made in over half of the residences, but fewer than half of the residences' dormitories had curtains or shades. Rugs on the floor were rarely seen. Over two thirds of the buildings had no rugs at all in these rooms.

In two thirds of the buildings, bathrooms had to be used by a minimum of ten residents. In one case there was one bathroom for 31 residents and in another one for 59 residents. In over two thirds of the buildings, each shower had to be shared among six or more residents. In one building there was one shower only for 70 residents. Under these circumstances bathing could hardly be a private activity. The possibility of this was even further restricted, since in only four buildings were there showers with curtains or partitions available to be shared by no more than two residents. In 71 per cent of the buildings none of the showers were partitioned or curtained off. Urinals and toilets were equally unprivate places for most residents. In 17 (81 per cent) of the buildings there were no doors on any of the toilets. Amenities like mirrors and toilet paper in these areas were also rare. While in 52 per cent of the bathrooms there were mirrors and in 48 per cent toilet paper was available, there were five buildings where there were no mirrors in the bathrooms, and one third of them where no toilet paper was available. It is clear from this summary that provision of amenities for daily living in the physical environment was very uneven across the 21 residences. What this means for a resident can best be understood by contrasting the quality of life for residents in terms of these features of their environment in the best provided-for building and the least provided-for building.

In Building 14, with a score of 33 on the IPE, the day rooms were reasonably well furnished. There was one armchair for every two residents and a settee for every eight. There were a number of occasional tables, one for every four residents, and a similar abundance of waste paper baskets. The rooms had curtains at their windows and when the residents sat down to watch television no more than twelve need view the same set. These living rooms were by no means luxurious but they were passably comfortable. Upstairs the residents' beds were in dormitories, 13 in each, but within these rooms attempts had been made to personalise the space as much as possible. Every resident had a locker by his bed and there was a wardrobe available for each of them as well. Each dormitory had different coloured bedspreads in it. Half of them were decorated with posters, and all of them had curtains at the windows. No more than six residents had to share a bathroom, and in each of them there was a shower and a handbasin. All of the showers had curtains and partitions and there was a mirror in every bathroom. There was a toilet in each of these bathrooms with toilet paper provided. While conditions in the living rooms in this building were hardly luxurious, the residents' sleeping areas and those in which they bathed were ones in which some personalised care and privacy were a possibility.

By contrast in Building 9, which scored two and a half times higher than Building 14 on this index of care, the living rooms had only one positive feature, namely the availability of armchairs. There was one of these for every two residents, but there was only one couch for every 35 residents and occasional tables for just as few. Even if the residents could have somehow all managed to sit down in these rooms there was no television for them to watch at all and none of the rooms had curtains. Jagged, torn screens covered windows which looked out on 'the porch', a barren concrete area surrounded by a wire fence.

There were two resident dormitories in this building, each with 18 beds and very little else. There were no bedside lockers at all, nor wardrobes. None of the rooms had shades or curtains at the windows and the floor was bare concrete. The beds did have different coloured spreads on them, but this hardly affected the overall bleak, unpersonalised quality of these rooms at all.

Each dormitory had its own bathroom and there was one handbasin for 18 residents. Three showers were available for the residents in each dormitory, but none of them had curtains or partitions, and none of the toilets available to them had toilet paper. Bathing was a public event, and even if a resident wanted to look at himself in a mirror in these rooms, he could not. It is difficult to convey in words the cheerlessness of such a barren physical environment. The residents here, aimlessly rattling from empty room to empty room, at times seemed like so many dried leaves in the wind.

Contacts with the Community

As can be seen from Table 8.1, the scores on the Index of Community Involvement (the ICI) also show a wide range. Scores on this measure could range from zero to 48, the lowest score indicating that everyone in a residence had been involved in the past month in each of the community activities listed on the measure. The range in Institution A on this measure was from 13 to 48, with a mean score of 36.8 and a standard deviation of 11.3. When we looked at the unit scores on this measure in this institution using a one-way analysis of variance, we found that being part of a unit seemed to have no significance for the extent to which residents in buildings were involved in these community-based activities ($F_{3;4} = 0.46$, ns). The mean scores for each unit are given in Table 8.6.

Table 8.6: ICI Scores, Mean and Standard Deviation, Institution A

	Unit 1	Unit 2	Unit 3	Unit 4
Mean	32.3	32.8	46.5	40.5
Standard Deviation	12.5	13.3	2.1	10.6

The scores on this index in the other eight buildings studied were within the range found to characterise the 13 buildings in Institution A. Involvement in the community was clearly least in the four buildings studied in Institution C, but there was still no significant difference between the mean scores of the buildings in these three settings. With the inclusion of these eight buildings, the overall mean for the 21 residences rises to 39.3, with a standard deviation of 9.6.

Contact with the surrounding community was not a common experience for the majority of residents in these 21 settings. Over all, only 16.6 per cent of them had been out shopping in the last month; 22 per cent to the cinema, three per cent to a museum, 17 per cent on a bus ride and 24 per cent to a restaurant. Fewer than ten per cent had been to a church of one kind or another, or the hairdresser, or to visit someone other than their parents. About a quarter of the residents (28.4 per cent) had been on an overnight visit to their families, friends, or other relatives, and on a holiday with the family (29 per cent). Vacations organised by the institutions had only involved ten per cent of the residents in the past year. The most common experience was a car ride, in which 31 per cent of the residents had been involved during the preceding year. Morris (1969) reports that the number going on holiday in her

survey varied between 10 and 25 per cent, and that three quarters of
her sample never went home. Over all, somewhat more of the residents
we studied did go home and did go on holidays but whether you did or
not depended not on what school or hospital you lived in, but in what
residence within these you were domiciled. We can again compare the
'best' residence on this index of care with the 'worst' to get some flavour
of what variation on this scale means.

Building number 7 (score = 13) and number 21 (score = 48) both
housed moderately to mildly retarded people. In the former there were
27 men, and in the latter 76 women. All of the men in Building 7 had
been to a film, and to the barber, as well as on a bus and car ride in the
last month. All of them had been to a restaurant during the same period
of time. By way of contrast none of the ladies had been to see a film or
on a car or bus ride in the past month, and only four of them had been
to a hairdresser in the community. (All the institutions had their own
hairdressing services.) Eighty per cent of the men had been out shopping
and to a religious service. None of the ladies had been to the latter,
and only seven per cent of them had been out shopping. Eighty-eight
per cent of the men had been on a vacation organised by the staff in
the past year whilst only four per cent of the ladies had been able to
enjoy such an experience. Twenty per cent of the men had even been
to a museum in the previous month, and 16 per cent had actually
visited people in their own homes other than their parents. None of the
ladies had done either of these. A family vacation was a relatively rare
experience for the men (twelve per cent had been on one in the past
year) but it was not part of life for any of the ladies.

These two illustrations indicate that, within the limits described by
the scale scores, contact with the community entailed quite substantial
differences in the experience of the residents of these 21 buildings.

Discussion

In this chapter, we have attempted to describe the range in the quality
of care we observed in these institutions regarding four aspects of resident
life – the care-taking of daily events, staff speech, the physical environment, the community experience. We have already explained in Chapter
3 why we shall use only our data from the RRMP and the ISI to explore
the relationship between care and other characteristics of these settings.
The choice of these two measures in no way implies that we think the
areas measured by the IPE and the ICI are unimportant. As we have
pointed out, the IPE is measuring a dimension of care which is independent
of that measured by the RRMP, though somewhat related to the pattern-

ing of staff speech. The significance of the physical environment in terms of the stimulating effects it can have on the residents ought not to be underrated or ignored, even if improvements will involve spending money. Levy and McLeod (1977) have demonstrated that an improvement in the physical environment can produce 'appropriate and productive behaviour for institutionalised children' (p. 28). They set about enriching the physical environment of a ward for profoundly and severely mentally handicapped children, observing the children's behaviour systematically both before and after the environmental changes were made. Their findings are fascinating, not least because they show a differential use by the children of the amenities they introduced. They noted that there was a reduction in the amount of neutral and stereotyped activity engaged in by the children after these spatial changes were made and the amenities introduced, a reduction that was statistically highly significant.

We have noted that there are marked deficiencies in the physical environment in many of the residences we studied. This environment is shared by residents and staff. We think it is unstimulating for both of them. Tizard (1964) has pointed out that if staff are comfortably and adequately accommodated and content then the residents in their care will be better looked after. We have some supportive observations to make on the matter of the staff's contentment (see Chapter 11), but we are sure that he is right in his observations about the importance of pleasant physical surroundings for the staff also.

The ICI did not measure a dimension of care which was statistically independent of that measured by the RRMP, but clearly it provides data about aspects of the residents' lives which are not directly included on the RRMP. Balla (1977) has argued that 'more involvement with the community is better' (p. 118). We think so too. The overall extent of such contact in these settings, as we have remarked, was not high. We can find little to commend, as far as care is concerned, when only 15 per cent of all the residents we studied had been out shopping in the last month, and less than one third for a car ride. Such simple everyday activities ought to be as much a part of the residents' lives, we think, as they are of our own.

Because we think they are of significance in terms of policy issues, we note here our findings about the relationship between these two measures (the IPE and the ICI), and the average IQ of the residents within a building. Both the scores on the IPE and the ICI were highly correlated with average resident ability. The less able got less of everything: fewer armchairs, fewer toilets, and fewer lockers. Chances to visit places

outside the institution were markedly greater for the less disabled. As
we have noted, very insignificant proportions of the residents had had
community contact of *any* sort in the month preceding our research.
But even within these limits, differences could be seen in the frequency
with which such contacts were experienced by the residents which were
clearly linked to the average IQ level of the building population. Thus in
Buildings 9, 10, 11 and 17 for example, none of the residents had been
shopping in the last month. Nor had any of the residents in the first three
of these buildings been on a bus ride in this period. All these buildings
accommodated profoundly and severely retarded people. By contrast,
in Buildings 1, 3, 7 and 14, more than half the residents had been shopping and on a bus ride in the past month. It may be difficult to involve
more severely handicapped people in these types of activities but it is
not impossible, as is clear from the fact that in Building 12, where 30
profoundly and severely retarded ladies lived, all had been to the movies
in the past month as well as on a car ride, and over half of them had been
to a restaurant for a meal. In Chapter 10, we will have some further
comments to make on these associations between care and resident
ability level. The magnitude and consistency of these correlations raises
difficult and important questions about the provision of care for the
more severely handicapped in these institutions. The bias in resource
distribution reflected in the results for the IPE and the ICI particularly
suggest that this deprivation of the more disabled may well be a matter
of deliberate policy. If so, the rationale for these policies of resource
allocation surely needs explicit consideration, as we discuss at more
length in Chapter 10. First, however, we provide in Chapter 9, for comparison with our numbers and tables, some descriptions by the residents
themselves of the quality of their environments.

9 SOME COMMENTS FROM THE RESIDENTS

We have just described how the residents were cared for by presenting data about the four dimensions of care we measured with our research instruments. Along with the numerical data we sketched, as well as we were able, some brief images of the meaning of these numbers for the lives of the residents. Now we present some observations by the residents themselves about their lives and the conditions of care they experienced. We have described how we obtained these resident writings briefly in Chapter 1.

Our writers had much to say, some of it critical, some of it not, but all of it indicating that they were clearly very much aware of the world around them. We begin with a selection of their observations about the day-to-day care they were provided with. In each case, we provide as background a brief description of the writer, and present the material as they wrote it.

Two young women living at the same institution wrote descriptions of life in their residences. The first, by C.D., demonstrates the complexity of the relationships between staff and residents. C.D. is 25 years old and has been a resident for 12 years. She has a job in the state school and likes music. The second piece is by N.M., who is 32. She has been a resident since she was 6½ years old. She enjoys arts and crafts and caring for plants.

> I am in Blue Hall, and I act up sometimes. Sometimes I feel like taking LSD or killing myself. Sometimes because I dont think people really care for me at all. They just say it to make me believe them . . . I cut myself with a razor blade and wrote peace and love with it too. I give the attendants trouble sometimes too. I tell them like it is. And I am afraid to go out because of what happened when I did live out with foster homes and how they worked me. I am really incredibly scared to leave this place. You better believe it too. I never want to leave my favorite attendant; and no one is going to try to fool me or play tricks either, not no more. They did it too many times already. Now they better just think twice now. I want to live with this attendant so very badly, really I do too. You can't go anywhere alone either you have to go with someone. I do hate to go alone by myself anywhere really I do too. When we have showers they are in

there with you. We have no privacy at all. Wherever we go to attendants have to go with us we can't go without attendants they go where we go. Like to the movies or the grounds or parties like those for Christmas they go with us too. They count us when we go anywhere. They sometimes fight with you when you are telling the truth. They never take our word at all; that I mean too. Like when attendants are saying things to us and start on us, the head one does not believe the girls at all; they believe the attendant all the time.

You have to go to bed at 10.0 o'clock every night. If there was a good show on TV they would not let us see it either. We cannot go in the office or we will get a black mark. If we go in anyone's ward we will get a black mark too. Even if we went in to give someone something you have to ask like a little baby. Really it is really stupid really it is honest. You have to go in the dining room if you eat or not. Even if you are not eating in the dining room you have to sit for the ones that are.

The second piece, by N.M., expresses vividly the toll residential life takes over the years of a woman's life.

When I was 6½ I came to this school I learn now to read and write and play with other children I also learn how to make my bed and wash dishes. When I turn a seven year old I knew how to get around the school and learnt that I could not have everything my way. By the time I was 8 years old I learnt every thing a little girl could know. At 9 years old I was punished for what I done wrong. . . Once a month we got to see our family and that was all. For a long time we not go home only once a month.

Later in my life I got to know that I could not do what I wanted. I had to do what the nurses ask to do and had to tell them where I was going at all times. At seventeen years old I ran away from the school and when I came back I was punished for what I did and if I ever had any children I would never put them in this school . . . Someday I hope to see the school close down.

It is not a good place to live in, there are bugs in here and I don't like it. It is not very healthy. I like helping people and working around little children. I like making pictures and I like doing art.

L.C. had only recently come to live in one of the state schools we studied. He plays the guitar and enjoys folk music and reading. He is 31 years old and had been in state schools for 9 years, ever since he was 22.

His description of an incident which had occurred in his residence tells us not only about his feelings, but also something of the different attitudes of the attendants, the physical environment he lived in, and the problems of sharing it with others.

It was night. It was time to go to bed. Some of the boys helped out the boys in wheelchairs to get undressed. They all went to bed. There were two men and lady on that night. (Attendants on duty.) They turned the TV around in the opposite direction so that the men could watch it, and the boys could sleep. Of course the next day the morning shift was talking about it. Of course, I was listening too. The TV was moved out of 33 (the ward) all the way down to the hall to the office downstairs.

The boys looked up there was no TV. What had happened to it? They were talking about it in the office. One of the attendants was mad because it wasn't that man's TV. He had no right touching it. A friend and I watch sometimes. They took the TV back to ward 1. All the boys in ward 1 could watch it. They'll never try that again. Now me and my friend can watch it.

C.V., who is 44 years old and has been a resident at a state school for 15 years, had some positive comments to make on her day-to-day life there. She had just been moved to a new residence and goes to evening classes in the community, making her own way from the institution to get there.

I moved over here to Halfway House. I like it very much. More than Yellow House, it was too noisy. I like living here with the boys, and I can go out at night time. I couldn't go out before, and I thought I was old enough. I go to movies and entertainments.

The boys are helpful and we have coffee together and sometimes pizza. I like to cook. I am 44 years old. It's about time I learned how to cook a good meal.

Perhaps we should say that the Halfway House to which she referred had the most resident-oriented score on the RRMP of all the residences we studied.

Several of the residents made comments about their contacts with the community, or the lack of these. We quote from 5 of them. The first piece is by L.P. who is 76 years old. He has lived in the state school since he was 6 years old. He likes to keep busy, he told us, and still helps out

with the chores in the residence in which he lives: 'The people around
this place won't let me go and see my friends. I'm supposed to see
them once a week. I was supposed to see them a week ago yesterday. I
haven't had any mail from them in a long while. They're supposed to
give me a television set. My friends don't come out very often. I don't
get mail very often.'

The second piece is by M.S., who is 34 and has lived in the state
school for almost five years. He told us that he enjoys reading the news-
paper and typing letters. He wrote us a piece which he entitled 'My
cerebral palsy weekend at Cape Cod'.

I go to Cape Cod every winter for nothing. The owner of the hotel
gives us the whole hotel to 'The United Cerebral Palsy of Greater
Boston'. We have a good time. We go by bus. We go on a Friday; we
come back on a Sunday. We go swimming. We have all kinds of danc-
ing. We go on trips to see the Cape.

The owner of the hotel cannot do it in the summer because he is
so busy with the other people that go to the Cape in the summer, and
the price is much higher in the summer, than it is in the winter, and in
the summer is when the owners of all of the hotels on the Cape make
their money. And while we are at the Cape, we eat good.

The third piece is by F.M., who is 57 years old and has lived in one
state school for 46 years. She works in one of the residences and told
us that she enjoys listening to the radio and watching television.

It costs a lot of money to live on the outside. I know for a fact it
does, you pay for gas. I'll tell you, you pay for the clothes too, and
a place to live, they'll come and take it away house and all, lights
and all, if you don't pay. I don't think its fair at all out in the world.
If I was president of the United States, I'd give the people more
income tax money. Every Thursday somebody at the bank should
give you a cheque to pay your bills.

If you don't work you don't get paid. That way you don't get a
cheque, and if you don't get a cheque you can't pay for the house
and the lights and then you are out in the cold, and that aint so good
either. So if you live outside you've got to have a job or they'll bring
you back here and that's not so good either. Here you don't have to
pay for your bills. Outside you have to pay for everything and that
way its good to live here.

The fourth piece is by M.K. who is 32 years old and has been a resident for 25 years. She wrote the following for us, which she entitled 'My Family'.

I miss them. My sister Winnie, and Betty and Nora. And my aunt and little nephews, too. I miss them, too.

They took me in the car. They got a new car. But I don't know how they'll get here. Maybe they don't know where this building is.

I'd like something like a card. Just some mail to send to me. To ask me how I am.

I miss my mother and father now. But I can't see them now 'cause they're up there in heaven.

But sometimes I get upset. When there's a noise, I get upset. And I'm trying as good as I can to be good and to help out.

A.M. is 71 and has been in the state school in which we found him since he was 15. He told us this tale of his excursion into the big city.

In Boston I got lost. Men took boys (the residents) to ball game. In the Boston metro elevator I got in crowd and man in front of me said 'the other boys gone'. Gee I says. He said 'you from the school: you lost?' I went to store, lost 1.00 in the morning.

He said you got money supper time. 'I'll call get you coffee. I call police.' He said 'How old are you Sonny?' I said 71. He said, 'you want something to eat?' He said 'stay there; 2 men come take you to police station'. The judge said 'You wait here, watch TV'. All the policemen, waiting on me, giving something to eat. They said 'How long you lived there?' I said 50 years. We all sat around talking. They said 'First time you been here?' I said, yes. They showed me around and the school cop came and got me. I had a good time getting lost on trolley car.

Finally, we close this section with a piece by S.S. who is 29 years old. She has lived in the state school since she was 9 and currently works in the coffee shop there, as well as attending night school at the local high school. Her description of two administrators, entitled 'The Main Office', needs no further comment.

Dr Hill sits and reads with his feet on the table at the edge. He needs something to rest his feet on. Something soft. His feet get tired cause he works so hard in the office doing reports. Reports on different people all over the school.

He don't have any foot stool, but he needs one. His job is awful hard. When boys and girls have a lot of problems on their mind they go to see Dr Hill to help them.

I wish he would come down here to see how we act, not yelling or screaming or hollering. And that way he could get more exercises for his feet. And they wouldn't get tired from sitting.

Him and Dr Lane are both friends. The bank book I get now I'm going to need. Dr Lane helped tell how much money I can take out. Dr Lane works hard too on reports.

And he never sits still for 5 minutes. He needs to sit down for awhile. All the running around might be too much for him. I wish he would come down to our workshop and see how we do down there.

Dr Hill and Dr Lane are doing real good down in the main office running this place.

Part Five

FACTORS AFFECTING CARE

10 THE RESIDENTS

The structure of an organisation reflects the way in which the tasks it is established to perform are shared out amongst its participant members, and the lines of authority and responsibility established to ensure that these tasks are achieved. However, the work to be done must partly mould and shape the carrying out of the tasks. To a considerable extent the residents, for whom and with whom much of the work in these institutions has to be done, generate the tasks presented daily to the direct-care staff.

We have noted the considerable variations among residences in the same institution in the provision of care. One of the other most striking differences amongst these residences was in the people who lived in them. The residents varied in their age, sex and functional ability, and there were different numbers of residents living in these buildings. These variations provided us with an opportunity to examine how differences in each of these factors corresponded to the variations in care which we found to exist within the three institutional settings.

In this chapter we shall examine the way in which the residents themselves influenced the work of the direct-care staff.

Age and Sex of Residents

Neither age nor sex of the populations in the residences were significantly associated with our measures of the quality of care. All our buildings housed adult populations, so that the range in average age of the populations was somewhat restricted. Nevertheless, across an age span from 16 to 56, resident age was not related to either the RRMP Scale, or the ISI scores. Ten of the buildings were exclusively female, nine were male, and two were mixed. Again, tests showed no significant differences between male and female populations on either of these two measures of care.

Functional Ability of the Residents

To study the effects of resident functional ability we decided to use an IQ measure derived from an average of the most recent IQ scores available in the institution records for each resident in the buildings. We do not believe that IQ tests are necessarily a fully adequate measure of 'functional ability'. We have serious reservations about the use of IQ tests (Pratt & Hall, 1977), and current definitions of retardation (e.g. by the AAMD) reinforce this point by requiring the use of additional diagnostic tools beyond the IQ test. However, the tests were convenient for research purposes here, because we were working with a wide range of competence, so that even rather crude estimates of population differences were useful. Also, these measures had been used by the administration to effect the 'functional' grouping of the residents. We collected data from the attendant staff regarding each resident's functional, academic, linguistic and social behaviours, as we have already described. In Chapter 3 we noted that these staff reports were highly correlated with tested IQ (correlations in the .70 to .90 range), with the exception of behaviour problems. In the absence of more adequate data on resident competence, we reluctantly settled for IQ scores as a measure of 'functional ability'.

The wide range of functional ability characterising the populations in the study has already been described in Chapter 5. In Table 10.1 we use the AAMD standard criteria for levels of handicap to summarise the situation (Grossman, 1973). Four of the residences have a population falling primarily in the profoundly retarded range (IQ 19), four in the severe range, eight in the moderate range, and five primarily contain residents who would be designated as mildly retarded by this criterion.

Table 10.1: Distribution of Functional Ability by AAMD Levels of Handicap

Level of Handicap	IQ Range	Building Nos from sample
Profound	0-19	9, 10, 11, 17
Severe	20-35	6, 12, 15, 20
Moderate	36-51	1, 2, 4, 8, 13, 14, 16, 21
Mild	52-68	3, 5, 7, 18, 19

Do care practices in these different settings vary with resident competence? King *et al.* (1971) observed no relationships of this sort in a group of English facilities for the retarded. McCormick *et al.* (1975), however, in a cross-national study, found that more severely handicapped residents were more likely to get less resident-oriented care. Our results are consistent with the findings of McCormick and his colleagues, and hold, as we have noted, across all four of our indices of care. There is a

very strong relationship between the quality of care and resident competence levels: the less able get less in every way.

For the RRMP Scale the correlation between average resident IQ
and the quality of care was very high ($r = -.84$, $p < .01$). Residences with
less competent populations were consistently characterised by more
institution-oriented care-taking: practices like lining up; rigid time scheduling, and high staff/resident social distance. For our ISI measure of
staff talk to residents the correlation with resident IQ across the 21
buildings was ($r = +.59$, $p < .01$), somewhat lower, but still substantial.
The less competent the residents, the less frequent the amount of stimulating talk by the staff to them. And a more detailed look at the *same*
direct-care workers, addressing either more or less competent groups of
residents, showed these same differences in the frequency of informative speech (Pratt *et al.*, 1976). This latter finding documents clearly
that it is differences amongst the residents which provide different
'situations' for the staff care-takers, and which in turn are related to
differential care-taking behaviours. Similar findings have been reported
since we completed this work. Grant & Moores (1977), observing staff
and residents interact on two wards of two hospitals for the mentally
handicapped in England, found that it was residents 'with a low vocab-
ulary age, low assessed levels of independence, and high assessed levels
of social maladaption' (p. 263) who were least involved in verbal interaction initiated by the staff. The less able, it appears, lose out in England,
as they do in Massachusetts, USA. While this framework is neat and tidy,
it is too simple. It leads to the impression that less stimulating care is
inevitable for less competent residents. It could be argued this is because
they 'evoke' a less stimulating reaction from any care-taker. It seems to
suggest that by virtue of their current behavioural deficits, severely
handicapped residents inexorably have to be managed differently from
more able peers. The management we are describing is that of daily recurring events. If this argument is valid, it implies that profoundly
retarded individuals, merely by virtue of their being such, have to get
up at the same time seven days a week, 365 days a year, and go to bed
in a similarly regimented fashion. They cannot have their own clothing.
If they go out for walks, they must always go *en masse*, in the company
of like-situated others. They must always wait after a visit to the toilet
until everyone else there is found to be ready to leave. By and large
when they are spoken to by direct-care staff they must be denied the
normal chit-chat of conversation and hear only orders to do this or not
to do that. We recognise that the tasks involved in caring for the
profoundly and severely retarded are in many ways harder for the

direct-care staff than those involved in caring for the more able mentally handicapped. Responses are often rare from the residents and behavioural increments infrequently seen. But it seems to us the essence of illogicality, rather than the inexorable consequence of the residents' attributes *per se*, that their care be characterised by unstimulating and rigid management. This can only underline their similarities, rather than their individuality. The environments thus generated are not only arid for the residents but also for the staff who work with them.

The differences in resident management on the RRMP and the ISI, which are so clearly associated with the residents' functional ability, are very unlikely to be 'caused' solely by differences in this characteristic of the residents. As we noted in Chapter 8, we found the same association between lower level IQ and paucity in the availability of physical amenities within the buildings themselves. Surely the presence of mirrors in the bathroom, of waste bins, and of curtains in the living rooms is not inevitably controlled by the residents' functional ability. Variations in physical amenities provided seem clearly a part of discretionary policy, readily subject to alternative allocation. Yet the distribution of these resources in the buildings is strongly correlated with average resident IQ ($r = +.88$, $p < .01$). The more severely retarded the residents, the less they get in the way of such facilities. Many everyday conveniences, such as wardrobes or lockers, were simply not part of life in many of the residences for the severely handicapped. Not only are the residents deprived as a consequence of this inequable distribution of physical resources but the direct-care staff working in these buildings clearly have less in the way of resources available to them to generate a resident-oriented environment. It is difficult to keep personalised clothing, for example, if you work in residences where lockers and wardrobes are either totally unavailable, or there for some small proportion of the population.

To summarise, resident ability (as indexed by mean IQ level) is strongly associated with RRMP and ISI scores (as well as IPE and ICI scores), while resident age and sex are not. At a process level, it seems most sensible to consider this as evidence of the impact of resident handicap on the care-taking behaviour of the direct-care staff. Less competent residents provide a different 'environment' for their care-takers than do the mildly retarded, and this in turn is associated with a different quality of care by staff. In a wider sense, however, this interpretation must be seen as conditioned by the general context in which these processes occur. Here the context was (*a*) an institutional policy which promoted homogeneous grouping by level of resident competence, and (*b*) an inequitable allocation of amenities and opportunities to the more handicapped. These seem to us to be|high-risk strategies for institutional care, in that groups of more disabled residents may elicit quite custodial care almost 'automatically' in such an impoverished milieu. These strategies appear to produce arid environments for both severely retarded residents and the staff who care for them. Surely these two policies, widely prevalent in residential facilities, deserve close scrutiny and some close investigation of alternatives before we confine our more disabled charges to the kinds of environment we have described.

Under current conditions in these institutions it may be harder to provide stimulating care for the severely and profoundly retarded but nothing in our research indicates that it is impossible. The deliberate policy of functional grouping enabled us to observe some of the delet-erious consequences of this for the care of the severely and profoundly retarded. It did *not* give us an opportunity to study directly the effects of alternative grouping policies. Other approaches are clearly possible. A classic example is provided by the research of Skeels (1966), and a more recent one by that of Kushlick and his colleagues (1975). The former described the beneficial effects of allowing mildly retarded adult women to foster young retarded children. Kushlick has made it clear that groups of children who span a wide spectrum in terms of their functional ability can be accommodated together, and all can be provided with individualised and stimulating care. There may be diminishing returns for the more able retarded at some point, if mixed ability group-ings are cared for together. That possibility can be empirically evaluated. What is clear now is that for the severely retarded, homogeneous function-ally based groupings generate an environment in which direct-care staff consistently provide care which is characteristically unstimulating, un-differentiated, de-personalised, and rigid. Efforts to change this have to involve altering policies at the institutional level. New policy must reflect a philosophy not of separate and worse for some, but a more positive approach to the use of available resources both physical and human, to meet the needs of all of the resident population.

Numbers of Residents

The residences we studied varied widely in population size, from 21 to 92. It is a truism, though not always an accurate one, that individualised attention is harder to provide in larger groups. Other recent studies have suggested that management practices in institutions for the retarded are more custodial in large living units (e.g. McCormick *et al.*, 1975). Our evidence is similar. The correlation between building population size and the RRMP Scale scores among our 21 residences indicated that in the larger residences the daily management of the residents tended to be more institution-oriented ($r = .50$, p$<$.05). However, ISI scores were not significantly associated with size ($r = -.26$). This suggests that the impact of total numbers is, reasonably enough, confined to residence-wide policies, rather than directly shaping minute-by-minute staff/resident interchanges. A look at the distribution here indicates that the association between the RRMP Scale scores and building population size is entirely due to the fact that the four residences with fewer than 30 people are invariably resident-oriented in their care practices. When population size varies between 30 and 90, this variation appears to be unrelated to RRMP Scale scores ($r = .10$). Thus in small living units, resident-oriented practices seem relatively easy to achieve. Living units with 30 or more residents in them are much more variable in the kind of care provided there: a building with 59 residents scored 43 on the RRMP Scale, one with 92 residents scored 22, whilst a building with 75 residents scored 40 on this scale and another with 70 residents scored 28 on the same measure. Something approximating relatively individualised care is clearly possible in buildings with more than 30 residents, but the management of daily recurrent aspects of the residents' care *never* reaches the individualised levels we found to exist in buildings with fewer than 30 residents. It should be noted that other aspects of care, as measured by our index of community involvement and our index of the physical environment, were found to be completely independent of the numbers of residents in a building, just as we found true of the speech of the direct care staff.

Of course, the total building population is not really a way of measuring the size of the group with which a staff member is characteristically working. Usually the larger residences had many more staff. A better index of average group size is the staff/resident ratio of a residence, a common index of the level of staffing resources available. When we computed this ratio for each of our residences as we have already pointed out, we found that in general direct-care staff were indeed a scarce commodity. On the average, each staff member was responsible for about nine residents during his or her tour of duty. At best this ratio was about 1:4; at worst it rose to 1:18 in three of the buildings. While there was some tendency for residences with more handicapped populations to have a better staff/resident ratio, it was not very substantial ($r = .30$), and some of the severely retarded populations had staffing ratios of 1:17 or 1:18. It is clear enough that in none of these residences is anything approaching a sustained one-to-one staff/resident situation possible.

Across the range of differences we did observe, there was no evidence that this staff/resident ratio was associated with the quality of care provided in the buildings (r = .06 for the RRMP, r = .17 for the ISI) on either of our measures of the quality of care, controlled for average resident IQ. This may seem surprising, but other studies have also suggested that the sheer level of staffing in these residential settings does not necessarily affect staff behaviour and care-taking (Tizard *et al.*, 1972; Harris *et al.*, 1974; Grant & Moores, 1977). Certainly this result can hold only within broad limits. A staff ratio of 1:1,000 is surely an automatic ticket to poor care or worse. However, providing individual-ised care is not merely a matter of adding more care-takers, though this is a popular point of view. We can explore this point in a little more detail with reference to the ISI.

In making our observations of staff speech to residents, we also recorded the social circumstances of each remark; that is, how many residents and staff were present at the time. These data permit us to consider some questions about the details of staffing patterns in relation to staff behaviour, in so far as their speech is concerned. Is it crucial to assign staff to a small group of residents to promote informative speech? The use of informative speech by staff appears to be independent of group size. When we compared this index in groups of five or fewer versus groups of six or more residents across all 21 buildings we found no significant differences (M = 30.8% *v.* 27.1%, t_{20} = 1.54, ns). This means staff are just as likely to make an informative remark when with a large group of residents, i.e. with more than five present, as with a smaller group. Similar results were obtained by Tizard *et al.* (1972) in residential children's homes in England. As the staff/resident ratio find-ings above suggested, staff behaviour seems not to be affected in any direct way by resident group size. Still, any particular resident will of course be spoken to more often in a smaller group, which may be the crucial factor of concern here. In that sense, group size is surely important.

What happens to the kind of speech the residents hear from staff when there are two or more members of staff available to care for them? Do direct care staff interact differently with residents when other staff are present? Yes, very clearly, our evidence suggests. The presence of more than one staff person systematically *decreases* the frequency of informative remarks to residents (32.0% *v.* 20.3%, t_{20} = 4.18, p<.001). Tizard *et al.* (1972) found the same effect we have just described in relation to staff speech to children in residential nurseries. Several other studies have indicated that the presence of more staff does not produce positive consequences for the care provided for the residents (Morris, 1969; Tizard, 1965; and Thormahlen, 1965). The most likely explanation for all these findings is that staff talk to each other instead of the residents when they can. Blindert (1975) actually observed that 'an increase in the number of staff in a situation signifies an increase in the number of interactions between staff on a topic not related to a client' (p. 40).

Of course, this does not mean that staff should always work alone to maximise their verbal interaction with the residents. There are undoubtedly many important reasons for having staff work in pairs or in larger groups, such as training of new workers, staff support, and various co-operative projects, for example. It does however seem apparent that simply adding more staff in an unplanned way is not an effective administrative strategy for improving the quality of care in these residential settings.

It could be argued that the presence of supervisors might more directly affect care-taking. We examined what happened to staff speech when a supervisor was present. In this case, the effects are less consistent and do not reach an acceptable level of significance, though the trend is in the same direction as that when other status-equal staff are present (24.6% $v.$ 17.8%, $t_{(10)}$ = +1.80 ns). Having your supervisor present may not consistently lower the quality of staff/resident interaction, but it certainly shows no indication of improving it.

General Comments

Two groups of college students, volunteers, play at a real-life game— 'prisoners' and 'guards'. Everybody knows it's only a game and, besides, nobody's a sadist or anything else deviant on the personality tests. But the game gets serious, the guards sometimes turn brutal and the prisoners vicious and, after a few days, the 'fun' has to be stopped.

This research by Zimbardo *et al.* (1975) is one of a number of disturbing recent studies demonstrating the power of the situation to determine behaviour—even behaviour we might usually think of as extreme or deviant. Most people, it turns out, will administer dangerous shocks to another, if someone with apparent authority tells them they should (Milgram, 1967). These are situations with 'high demand' characteristics. Personality, individual background differences and qualities—all these seem to pale as determinants of social behaviour when compared with the situation at hand. Indeed, much of recent social psychology can be described as a re-discovery of the power of the situation to evoke similar actions from different individuals (Mischel, 1973).

In this chapter, we have explored the immediate circumstances of care-giving for direct-care workers in institutions for the retarded. It is important to isolate these factors. They can tell us much about the structure of care-taking as a particular kind of social behaviour of tremendous applied relevance. Our results do seem, in some ways, to emphasise the power of the situation's 'demand' in determining care-taking behaviours, for example the effects of differing levels of client handicap on the care-taker. More subtly, the social circumstances of staff/resident interaction also appear to function as situational 'demands' governing behaviour.

Two points need making, however. One is that not *all* features of the situation are important to staff care-taking, at least as we measured it. Resident age and sex, for example, are not; but different levels of client handicap are. What does that mean? Surely that we need to go much beyond a simple description of immediate situational determinants, to try to specify the how and the why of their effects, and to say why some factors are important and other comparable ones are not.

The second point is related. Clearly the direct-care staff in these 21 residences were working in a variety of settings with different demand characteristics. The client characteristics that define the care staff's tasks are situationally specific but immediate circumstances are affected by behaviour within a wider context. A change in that wider context (e.g., general institutional policies) may lead to differences in the roles played by these more immediate factors. As we observed, the effects of resident handicap on care may well be shaped by the institutional policy of homogeneous grouping. A really adequate description and model for residential care-taking, then, will have to deal with these various levels of factors affecting staff behaviour, and provide ideas of how these levels are linked together. Though our later chapters make some very preliminary and tentative attempts to begin this, it is clear that this is a vast undertaking—one that cuts across traditional disciplinary boundaries and theoretical provinces. Perhaps we can do little more than acknowledge its importance at present. But such an acknowledgement should at least help us keep in mind the tremendous challenge of social theory and research applied to residential institutions.

11 THE DIRECT-CARE STAFF

A thorough review of research on the selection and training of attendants (the group we term the direct-care staff) was undertaken by Butterfield (1968). It is clear from this survey that the backgrounds and attitudes of these personnel have been considered to be of central importance in the care provided in institutions for the retarded. This group, as we have noted, constitute a majority of all institution employees. They have most contact with the residents (Fleming, 1962) and interpret the policies of the institution in their daily encounters with the residents. Much of the work that Butterfield (1968) reviews focuses on the personality characteristics of direct-care staff (Butterfield & Warren, 1962; Tarjan, Shotwell & Dingman, 1956, for example). Butterfield & Warren (1962, 1963), attempting to relate personality factors to attendant tenure, found 'no personality scales or pattern of scales that differentiated' those who left within a year of their appointment and those who stayed. Tarjan *et al.* (1956), although they did find some personality traits differentiated long- from short-tenured staff, found that the traits which differentiated the two groups in one institutional setting were not replicated in other settings. Butterfield, Barnett & Bensberg (1966) adopted another approach to the problem of understanding personnel turnover and instead of focusing on employee characteristics developed objective indices of the characteristics of institutions in a study of 26 such settings. They found six factors accounted for 80 per cent of the variance between the institutions and two of these factors, which they termed 'personnel turnover' and 'attendant working conditions' (p. 790) were independent of each other. They suggest that staff turnover, in addition to being influenced by job availability elsewhere, will be affected by 'intangible contributors to job satisfaction which were not tapped by the gross variables employed in the present study' (p. 791). The variables used in their study were the age of the institution, the salary of the attendants and the ratios of different groups of personnel to residents. All the data were obtained from a postal questionnaire completed by the superintendents of the institutions. This approach is unlikely to be sensitive to those 'intangible contributors to job satisfaction', to which they refer. Scheff (1961) has pointed out that the introduction of new programmes in mental hospitals, presumed to be therapeutic, has rarely taken account of the effects of ward settings. Neither, as far as we can see, have studies of direct-care staff attitudes and characteristics in institutions for the mentally retarded, whether to account for turnover or more immediately the care provided for residents. There is another major issue which the large number of studies on the characteristics of direct-care staff in institutions for the mentally retarded have not adequately addressed, and it is that of the relationship between expressed attitudes and actual performance.

As Butterfield observed in 1968, the research findings do not answer the question to what degree changes in direct-care staff's levels of knowledge and attitudes 'reflect themselves in their performance on the ward' with the clients (p. 323). It is not surprising that we still do not have an answer to this question for the seemingly transparent relationship between people's attitudes and their actual behaviour has been a difficult one to establish. A great number of studies on attitude-behaviour consistency over the years have suggested that people's verbal answers to questions about their views or feelings, and the way they behave in a particular situation, are often not closely related at all (e.g. Liska, 1974). A wide variety of factors seem to affect attitude-behaviour consistency, including, amongst others, measurement techniques and the social settings for behaviour. (Rokeach & Klieujunas, 1972; Fishbein & Ajzan, 1974). In organisational research, the classic review by Vroom (1964) documents the complexity of the relationships between employee satisfaction and job performance, and concludes: 'There is no simple relationship between job satisfaction and job performance.'

In this chapter, we will describe our efforts to study the relationship between a number of measures of the direct-care staff's backgrounds and work attitudes, and their care-taking behaviours. For each of these background and attitude factors, we have tested this relationship at two levels: first, a correlation between aggregate residence scores on the factor and our residence scores for the RRMP and the ISI and, secondly, an individual staff member analysis of the predictors of informative speech patterns to residents. This second analysis provides a way of testing the relationship between staff characteristics and care-taking performance more *directly*. Because we have relied on this second measure of individual performance a good deal in our interpretation of the evidence presented in this chapter, we felt a need to detail it here. Thus, the first section of the chapter briefly attempts to establish the credibility of this individual measure of staff speech performance. Subsequent sections then deal with background characteristics of direct-care staff as influences on the quality of care, and then staff work attitudes as another set of influences. A fourth section then provides a discussion of a model of staff 'institutionalisation', which attempts to account more systematically for the important effects discussed in the preceding sections. The chapter ends with a brief review of findings and policy implications.

Individual Performance and Attitude-Behaviour Consistency

As noted in Chapter 3, observations of staff speech in the residences were tabulated by individual care worker, thus allowing us to assess effects on individual performance, based on our questionnaire information for these direct-care workers.

Our sample for this part of the analysis had perforce to be small, for we could only use data derived from questionnaires for those staff for whom we also had observational data. Because of the times of day at which we collected our data on staff speech to residents, this meant that our sample had to be limited to the afternoon shift. Further, to ensure that we had a reliable estimate of individual amounts of informative speech frequencies, we selected from within this group only those staff for whom we had at least ten observational periods.

A total of 42 direct-care attendants who completed the questionnaires were observed speaking to the residents for the requisite number of observational periods. For each of these individuals the percentage of their speech to residents which was informative was calculated. This percentage became the index of performance for each individual staff member. The range amongst these attendants was from 0.0 per cent to 69.2 per cent, corresponding to the wide range between the buildings on this measure which we reported in Chapter 8.

[This group represented 33.6 per cent of all staff who responded to our questionnaire. Since only the afternoon shift (3.0-11.0 p.m.) staff were observed on the language schedule (approximately 50 per cent of all attendants), this represents a substantial proportion of all questionnaire respondents available. There is no reason to anticipate any possible bias in observational selection, since *all* staff who were on during specified periods in a building were always observed.]

A reasonable prediction regarding this index is that more stimulating speech to residents (as a behaviour) should be associated with more expressed positive concerns about the residents (as an attitude)—in other words that behaviour and attitudes should be consistent. As one way of validating our speech measure, we tested this prediction directly, using information derived from the questionnaire as an index of attitude.

At the end of our attendant questionnaire were two open-ended questions, which the respondent could answer in any way he or she chose: (*a*) 'What do you find to be the main problems in doing your job?' and (*b*) 'Are there things you would like to see changed here?' There was a wide variety of response to these questions. Some staff indicated no problems or changes at all, while others appended pages of often incisive and instructive comments. For present purposes, we developed, as described in Chapter 4, a simple coding system to indicate the presence or absence of a general 'concern' for the resident in these comments. Responses mentioning needs for more programmes, better treatment, more freedom and so on were classified as indicating such concern. Responses which excluded reference to such matters were classed as not manifesting direct concern for the resident. The responses of all staff members in our individual speech performance subsample – the 42 direct-care workers described above – were classified using this system.

Twenty-five (60 per cent) were judged to show a general concern for the residents and 17 were not. We wanted to control for the effects of the residence on the language measure, which ranged widely between buildings (see Chapter 3). To do this, we looked for all residences where we had some staff members with both types of attitude. We found nine buildings, with a total of 26 staff members which could be used for this test. When we matched the positive *v.* negative scorers across these nine buildings, we found that an attitude of general concern for the residents was associated with a greater frequency of informative remarks to residents (M = 39.0% *v.* 24.0% of all observations; $t_8 = 3.18$, p$<$.01). This matched sample test directly links variations in staff attitudes with staff behaviour, in a consistent fashion.

These results are quite straightforward; direct-care workers whose comments indicate a focus on resident needs are more likely to provide stimulating care. Yet, as we noted, such consistency is not always easy to determine and, as far as we know, this is the clearest indication of it in research studies on institutions for the retarded to date. It also suggests that our measure of staff speech is identifying a theoretically meaningful dimension of individual care-taking behaviour which is linked in a reasonable way to staff feelings. With this evidence in hand, we turn to a consideration of the effects of staff background on the quality of care.

Relationship between Staff Demographic Characteristics and Quality of Care

Our two measures of quality of care utilised for these analyses are the RRMP and the ISI (see Chapter 3 for a detailed description of these indices). Information about staff characteristics were obtained for each staff member from a voluntary questionnaire. From this source we derived aggregate indices for each of the 21 buildings in our study. For age, we used the percentage of staff in the building who were 30 or under; for sex our measure was the percentage of staff in the building who were female; our training measure was the percentage of staff who had undergone an in-service training programme; and finally, our length of service measure was the percentage of staff who had worked in the institution for less than one year. In Chapter 6, we described these demographic characteristics of staff in our three institutions; here we report on their relationship to the quality of care.

Parnicky & Ziegler (1964) have argued that if care is to be improved, staff selection procedures need amelioration. In their survey of institutional training of direct-care staff they concluded that poor selection methods present greater problems than the lack of training. If this is the case then the demography of staff is of more than academic interest.

Age. In order to assess the strength of the relationship between age of building staff members and quality of care, we correlated the percentage of direct-care staff in a building who were 30 or under with our two measures of the quality of care for the building. Because mean resident IQ is so highly correlated both with quality of care and with staff age (the lower the building mean IQ, the higher the percentage of attendant staff 30 or under), we statistically controlled for the effect of IQ on the relationship between age and quality of care. We found a statistically significant relationship existed: the larger the proportion of attendant staff in the building who are 30 or under, the more resident-oriented the care provided in the building, as measured by both the RRMP and the language index — see Table 11.1. We cannot conclude, however, that young people necessarily provide more resident-oriented care: we found four buildings, for example, in which more than 50 per cent of the staff were over 30 but which were characterised by quite individualised care. On the other hand, we also found buildings predominantly staffed by people 30 or under in which the care was institution-oriented. Furthermore, when we assessed *directly* the relationship between an attendant's age and his speech to residents, we could find no evidence in support of these trends. Staff members aged 30 or under do not address residents more 'informatively' than do older staff in the same buildings. This suggests that the relationship we found at the building level is mediated at the individual level by factors other than the attendant's age alone.

Table 11.1: Correlations Between Measures of Staff Characteristics and
Two Outcomes Measures for 21 Buildings[†]

Staff Characteristic	RRMP	Language Index
Age (% of building staff under 30)	-.67**	+.44*
Sex (% of building staff who are female)	+.20	+.42*
Length of service (% of building staff at the institution less than one year)	-.52*	+.21
Training (% of building staff with in-service training)	+.28	-.29

Notes:

[†]partial r's, controlling for level of resident handicap (IQ).
*p<.05, one-tailed.
**p<.01, one-tailed.

Sex. As with staff age, we assessed the relationship between sex and
quality of care by correlating building proportions with our two building measures of care, controlling for the effect of building mean resident
IQ. We found that the presence of a higher proportion of women among
the building staff is associated with a high amount of informative speech
with residents, but has no impact on resident care practices as measured
by the RRMP (Table 11.1). Once again, however, an analysis at the
individual level showed no consistent effect of staff sex on speech to
residents. Here too, as with age, it appears that the relationship at the
building level is mediated by some process, in the specific context of
the building, other than the actual staff characteristic itself.

Training. It is perhaps not surprising, in the light of the small numbers
of staff who had undergone any sort of training, as described in Chapter
6, that we found no significant relationships, either at the building or
the individual level, between staff training and quality of care (Table
11.1).

Length of Service. A stable building environment, with low turnover and
long-staying staff, could be assumed to make a positive contribution to
the quality of care provided residents. We had originally hypothesised
that the length of service of the attendant staff would have a significant

Table 11.2: Staff Length of Service by Informative Speech Performance[*]

Length of Service	3 mths	3-6 mths	6 mths -1 yr	1 yr- -2yrs	2 yrs- 5 yrs	5+ yrs
Above Building Median (N=34)	4	5	8	4	7	6
Below Building Median (N=32)	6	3	2	4	12	5

[*]The sample for this comparison is considerably larger because we collected this information on length of service from institution files on most staff who were observed in their work but did not return questionnaires.

association with the resident management practices of the building. We did indeed find such a significant association, but in the direction opposite from that expected: we found that the greater the percentage of staff in a building who have been at the institution less than one year, the more resident-oriented the care provided in that building (Table 11.1). In addition, this relationship was sustained at the individual level as well: longer-service staff tend to use informative speech less often than do shorter-service staff (see Table 11.1). Later in the chapter we discuss this factor in terms of a process model of staff institutionalisation.

We have found, in our investigation of the relationship between staff characteristics and the quality of care, some evidence that buildings characterised by younger, by female, and by shorter-stay staff tend also to be characterised by more individualised, resident-oriented care. But more importantly, we also found that, with the exception of length of service, these associations at the aggregate level were not sustained at the individual level: young staff do not provide more stimulating care than do older staff; women do not provide more individualised care than do men. It would be unwise to conclude, then, that changes in hiring practices—hiring more women or young people, for example—would necessarily result in more resident-oriented care. What these data do highlight is the need for further exploration of the relationship between individual and aggregate data, and particularly the situational variables that might influence the two. It is clear that further systematic exploration of how these various factors interrelate is strongly indicated. At the end of this chapter, we will discuss these issues in some detail. Now we turn to a consideration of our results regarding the impact of staff attitudes on care-taking.

Table 11.3: Average Number of Issues Attendants are Involved in
Deciding by Building

Building No.	Number of Issues
1	2.3
2	1.1
3	0.0
4	0.6
5	1.0
6	1.6
7	2.5
8	2.0
9	1.0
10	1.7
11	1.3
12	2.4
13	0.5
14	–
15	–
16	0.6
17	0.2
18	2.0
19	1.0
20	0.6
21	0.0

RRMP: $r_{partial} = .51^*$ ISI: $r_{partial} = +.45^*$

*$p < .05$, one-tailed.

Direct-Care Staff Work Attitudes and the Quality of Care

In this section, we look at four dimensions of the work attitudes of direct-care staff in these residences – decentralisation or feelings of participation in decision-making, the perceived formalisation of staff work roles, levels of communication with other members of the institutional organisation, and attitudes toward co-workers in the residence, or staff 'morale'. To study the relationship of these factors to care, we have used the RRMP Scale, as well as the ISI. The attendants' views of work are obtained from our questionnaire on work and personal background, given to all direct-care staff (see Chapter 4). [It will be recalled that we did not obtain data on these variables in 2 residences.]

1. Centralisation/Decentralisation. Direct-care staff in each building responded whether or not they thought that they (as a group) were 'usually involved in' decisions in three areas: (*1*) resident care, (*2*) domestic work, and (*3*) staff schedules. These three areas appeared to us to be directly relevant issues in the attendant's daily work life, in which he or she clearly had some stake. The number of 'yes' responses by each staff member was recorded, and an average obtained across all workers in the building for the number of areas in which staff perceived themselves involved in decision making. Table 11.3 shows this measure for each of the residences included in the analysis. The mean for all 19 buildings is 1.18, which suggests that workers perceive their involvement in these issues as rather low in general. In only three buildings did at least half of all respondents perceive themselves as involved in all three areas of decision making. Conversely, in eight buildings, more than half of all workers replied that attendants were involved in *none* of these decisions. Respondents were about equally likely to feel attendants are involved in decisions about work with the residents or domestic tasks, but were much less likely to report worker involvement in the scheduling of staff time — e.g. days off, vacations, and so on.

To investigate the relation between workers' perceived involvement and the quality of care, we correlated this index of staff decision making with each of the two primary measures of the quality of care-taking, across the 19 residences. Controlling for IQ and building size, we found that the level of association between this index and the RRMP Scale was r partial $= -.51$, ($p < .05$). Examining the same correlation for the index of informative speech, we again find a significant relationship ($r_{partial} = +.45$, $p < .05$). A higher average feeling of involvement is associated with more stimulating care for both our measures.

How does this overall relationship work for the individual staff member, we wondered. Are staff who feel some control over their work life more likely to provide stimulating care than staff in the same residence who don't? If so, this would suggest that feelings of control over work decisions could be a *direct* source of more stimulating care. Our results are consistent with this proposition, though only an actual intervention study could test its truth directly, of course. We found seven buildings where at least one attendant had scored 'high' on decision involvement (workers involved in two or three areas) and where at least one had scored 'low' (workers involved in zero or one area). When we contrasted the ISI performance scores for all high *v.* low scorers in these seven buildings, the means were significantly different (31.7% *v.* 18.3%, $t_6 = 2.02$, $p < .05$). Those staff who feel more involved in deciding work issues talk to the residents in their care in a more stimulating fashion. In fact, the main difference appears to be between workers who feel involved in all three issue areas, and those who don't (see Table 11.4). This suggests that

Table 11.4: Performance Scores on the Language Index and Degree of Decision Involvement

Number of areas involved in:	0	1	2	3
Mean Performance Score	23.0%	18.8%	25.9%	44.7%
(SD)	(17.9)	(12.4)	(24.2)	(12.8)
N	12	9	14	6

many workers who don't feel that they have a say in all immediately relevant job matters may in turn 'take it out' on the residents in their care, as Alutto & Acito (1973) suggest. Staff who felt deprived of decision-making power often made some harsh remarks on our question-naire: 'There is too great a division between "professional and admin-istrative" workers and attendants . . . Communication only comes from the top down—an "us" and "they" type of situation results, a power struggle with both moving further apart.'

'Many decisions are made by people outside of the building, who don't really take into consideration the feelings of in-building staff regarding the lives of residents and our relationships with them . . .'

'Nobody listens to us!'

Bogdan, Taylor, DeGrandpre & Haynes (1974) have argued that direct-care staff 'resent most professionals, supervisors and administrators' (p. 144). Our data suggest that this was true for some of these staff in the settings we studied. Surely this kind of alienation among line work-ers is not good for the organisation as a whole. Not unimportantly, as we have shown, it is not likely to be good for the residents these staff care for, either.

2. Formalisation. We asked staff members two questions concerned with how explicitly their jobs were constrained by formal specifications: whether they had written job descriptions and written rules about their work.

The written job descriptions which in principle they all received on their appointments, to which the direct-care staff were referring, are very general and vague. They are also focused on relatively 'custodial' aspects of staff duties, and emphasise aspects of physical care. We reproduce, to illustrate this, the job description which was available to the personnel of all of the institutions which described the position of attendant.

General statement of duties: Assists in the care of patients in a State Institution: performs related work as required.
Supervision Received: Works under the direct supervision of a nurse or attendant of higher grade who assigns and reviews work.
Examples of Duties:
1. Assists in the care of mental, tubercular, or other types of patient in a State Institution.
2. Bathes, feeds, shaves, dresses and attends to other needs of patients including administration of certain medication and treatments as prescribed and directed by professional staff.
3. Accompanies patients to and from the units of the institution.
4. Maintains housekeeping of assigned area including such duties as sweeping and polishing of floors, cleaning and dusting of beds, furniture, window sills, toilet and bathing facilities and the cleaning of walls.
5. Collects and delivers specimens to laboratory for analysis.
6. Cleans utensils and equipment on wards.
7. Assists in minor clerical work.
8. Instructs and trains patients in personal hygiene.

(Commonwealth of Massachusetts Civil Service Job Specification for Attendants.)

It was clear that there were wide differences among the staff regarding this dimension. For example, one staff member remarked: 'There is a lack of cooperation with some attendants, especially with the new help . . . we need rules that apply to everyone, not just a few.' A nice appeal to formalisation, indeed. In contrast, another worker complained about 'old rules that no longer apply or make sense'. As reports of the presence of written rules and written job descriptions were quite highly correlated with each other ($r = .45$, $p < .01$), it appeared reasonable as we noted in Chapter 4 to combine these two questions into a single measure of formalisation. So we calculated the percentage of staff in each residence who said that they had both written job descriptions and written rules. This composite index is shown in Table 11.5. The range among our buildings was as wide as possible on this variable, from 0 per cent to 100 per cent. Clearly there was no consensus about this issue.

We found partial support for the hypothesis that more formalisation

Table 11.5: Percentage of Staff Who Say They Have Both Job
Descriptions and Written Rules

Building No.	% of Staff
1	25
2	57
3	25
4	100
5	67
6	38
7	50
8	17
9	75
10	67
11	42
12	17
13	83
14	–
15	–
16	86
17	93
18	0
19	20
20	56
21	100

RRMP: $r_{partial}$ = +.16   ISI: $r_{partial}$ = -.42*

*$p < .05$, one-tailed.

(at least in the worker's perceptions) is likely to be an impediment to
care. The correlation with the RRMP Scale was not significant ($r_{partial}$
= .16). However, the association between this measure of formalisation and the ISI measure of staff-resident interaction was significant
in the predicted direction ($r_{partial}$ = -.42, $p < .05$). So it appears that residences in which staff are more oriented to written codifications of their
duties (ones which emphasise *custodial* aspects of work, we should
stress) are more likely to be characterised by low scores on the ISI. Again,
we tried to see whether this was because an individual worker who felt
these constraints was less likely to stimulate the residents in his or her
care. In the eight residences on which we could test this proposition,
where some staff said they had such rules and some said they did not,

there was a trend toward this result, but it was not significant (M = 23.3% *v.* 34.9%, t_7 = 1.37, ns). Here we are best advised to suspend judgement. It may be that such feelings of constraint are associated with less inform- ative speech patterns in this direct way, but we need more evidence to be able to say. Though our overall results do not provide much support for formalisation as an important factor in care, it may well be that our techniques of measurement were somewhat inadequate. Further explor- ation of this hypothesis seems warranted.

3. Communication. The virtues of 'effective communication' have become a positive fetish in our modern, increasingly fragmented and isolated society. Literally thousands of training programmes, paperback manuals, courses, and so on are based on the premise that nothing will help solve your problems or improve your situation like communicating. The research literature on residential institutions has echoed this pre- sumption, as a general rule (Stanton & Schwartz, 1954; Perrow, 1972, for example).

It is a little hard to fly in the face of this tide. Our results, however, suggest that simply getting together more frequently to talk about your problems with other concerned parties may not make all that much difference—at least to the provision of care. We studied attendants' reported frequencies of contact about resident problems with three other groups important to treatment programmes: other-shift attendants in the same building, professional workers, and the unit director. Our first finding here was that such contacts were fairly infrequent over all in the institutions (see Table 11.6); approximately once every two weeks with professionals and the unit director on the average. Perhaps this level of input shouldn't be expected to make much difference to staff care-taking. Anyway, it did not.

As Table 11.6 shows, frequency of contact with other shifts was un- related to either the RRMP Scale or the ISI. While there is a relationship in the predicted direction for frequency of professional contacts and the ISI (r = +.43, p<.05), the relationship of these contacts to the RRMP Scale is in the *opposite* direction to prediction (r = +.38, p<.10), though only marginal in significance. Furthermore, when the relationship between the speech measure and professional contacts is examined at the *indiv- idual* level, we again find that this direct relationship is negative. Staff who report more frequent professional contacts are less likely to inter- act in an informative manner with residents than staff in the same build- ing who report seeing professionals less often (M = 15.5% *v.* 34.1%, t_6 = -2.73, p<.05). Clearly, there is nothing here to support the notion that

Table 11.6: Average Frequency of Attendant Contact with Other Attendant Shifts, Professionals and Unit Director, by Building

Building No.	Other Shift	Professionals	Unit Director
1	3.8	3.0	3.3
2	3.6	2.4	2.7
3	2.8	2.3	2.8
4	4.0	2.8	3.0
5	3.0	1.5	3.0
6	3.9	2.5	3.0
7	4.0	3.0	3.0
8	3.8	3.3	3.2
9	3.8	2.2	2.7
10	3.8	2.0	2.3
11	3.6	1.7	2.5
12	3.9	1.9	2.4
13	3.2	2.8	(1.0)
14	–	–	–
15	–	–	–
16	3.6	1.4	3.1
17	3.9	2.6	3.2
18	3.0	4.0	3.0
19	3.4	2.2	2.0
20	3.0	2.0	1.4
21	4.0	3.3	2.0
RRMP: $r_{partial}$:	-.20	+.38	-.50*
ISI: $r_{partial}$:	-.02	+.43*	.01

*$p < .05$, one-tailed.

professional input (in the form of more frequent discussions with workers) has a direct beneficial impact on the care-taking behaviour of the staff member involved. We can think of a variety of ways of accounting, after the fact, for these conflicting results. But no simple model of just encouraging more 'communication' with professionals as the way to improve care in these institutions can find support in these results.

We did find (see Table 11.6) that frequency of contact reported with the unit director was positively related to more resident-oriented RRMP scores ($r = -.50$, $p < .05$). There was no trend for the ISI to be related to the level of these contacts, however. This was true at the individual level, too. Thus, while there is some support for the impact of greater unit director input on the treatment practices characterising the residence, there is no indication that this input affects staff/resident interaction styles directly.

To summarise, simply increasing the frequency of discussions about the residents between the direct-care worker and other members of the organisation shows little promise as a strategy for improving care (contact with the unit director may be an important exception). The general level of these contacts is low, which may be a source of their inefficacy. The role of specific kinds of communication also needs study. Perhaps certain kinds of training, or responding to particular concerns of the workers, would prove more effective. We did not attempt to study this. Our results simply tell us that just more talk is not enough.

4. Staff Morale. On our questionnaire, we asked each staff member to rate how 'helpful' other members of the building staff were. The respondent rated his or her feelings about this group on a five-point scale, from 'very helpful' to 'very unhelpful'. Table 11.7 shows the average percentage of respondents who rated this group as 'helpful' or 'very helpful' for the whole group of residences we studied. However, there are wide differences among the various residences on this attitudinal measure: the range for each group is from zero per cent or nearly so, to some buildings where *all* staff feel others are helpful. If we treat these attitudes towards co-workers as indices of 'morale', following Aiken & Hage (1966), the general level of alienation in these institutions must be characterised as quite high.

Are variations in these attitudes among the residence staffs linked to differences in care? Table 11.7 shows the correlations between this attitude variables and the two indices of the quality of care (controlled, as usual, for resident IQ and building size). These correlations are consistent and quite strong, though significant only for the ISI ($r = +.57$).

Groups who feel more positively about building co-workers are more likely to provide stimulating care. Schwartz (1957) has stressed the importance for the care of patients of high morale among care-taking staff.

Is the crucial factor here the *individual* worker's feelings about other staff? Apparently not. To test this, we compared workers high *v.* low on this index of co-worker attitudes for their performance on the ISI measure of speech to residents. We found eight buildings where some staff scored positively and some negatively on feelings about other workers. When we compared these positive *v.* negative scorers in these eight

Table 11.7: Percentage of Staff Rating Other Attendants as 'Helpful' or 'Very Helpful' in Their Work, by Building

Building No.	% of Staff Rating
1	50.0
2	14.3
3	25.0
4	100.0
5	66.7
6	50.0
7	100.0
8	50.0
9	41.7
10	66.7
11	45.5
12	71.4
13	66.7
14	—
15	—
16	57.2
17	28.6
18	100.0
19	20.0
20	30.0
21	25.0

RRMP: $r_{partial} = -.38$ ISI: $r_{partial} = +.57**$

**$p < .01$, one-tailed.

residences, however, we found no systematic differences in their speech performance at all (M = 23.5% $v.$ 21.0%, $t_7 = 0.31$, ns). It looks as if a particular worker's feelings about co-workers may not be *directly* relevant to his or her care-taking, but that in groups where more stimulating care is evident, workers also tend to feel better about each other.

Staff Institutionalisation: a Process Model

So far, we have shown that attitudes among direct-care workers vary a good deal, and that some are apparently associated with care-taking performance. An attitude of concern for the resident's needs, and the worker's perceived involvement in job-related decisions are the two clearest factors. Attitudes toward co-workers, formalisation, and level of communication with other organisation members seem less directly associated with care. But what differentiates direct-care workers who are high on these two attitudinal factors from workers who are low? And what can we make of this difference?

The residence setting itself appears to differentiate these attitudes considerably, of course. We have used this fact of variation between buildings as a tool to explore associations with care in this chapter. We will later be concerned with the organisational factors that may account for these differences between residences (see Chapters 12 and 13). But there is a general factor in these institutions involved too—and we will use it as a springboard to some discussion of a dynamic model of the institutional career of the direct-care worker in this section. That factor is the worker's length of service. Recall that this is the central demographic predictor of staff care-taking behaviour as well.

We noted that longer-service workers in the residences, those who had been at the Institute for more than one year, reported feeling more powerless about their work ($X^2 = 5.38$ p<.05) as shown in Table 11.8. Workers with this length of service also tended to be less resident-oriented in their concern for the residents, as indicated by their responses to the open-ended questions about their work, in the questionnaire they completed. It would be accurate to

Table 11.8: Staff length of Service and Perceived Participation in Decision Making

	Perceived participation in decision making		
	LOW	*HIGH*	
	(0.1 area)	(2, 3 area)	
Length of service:	%	%	
< one year	47	53	$X^2 = 5.38$
			(p < .05)
> one year	69	31	

describe the longer-service workers' lower likelihood of expressing concern about resident needs as part of a generally greater conformity to the current organisational situation. Schein (1968, 1971) has argued that 3 basic modes of adjustment to the organisation can characterise the individual worker—rebellion, creative individualism, or conformity. Further, he argues that these modes become increasingly important later in the individual's career with the organisation in question. Among the longer-service staff in our institutions of study, increasing levels of *conformity* seem evidenced by the tendency to report very few problems or suggestions for change at all on our open-ended questions (only 36 per cent of long-service staff mentioned two or more problems or concerns, compared with 75 per cent of the short-service staff, $X_1^2 = 13.9$, p<.001). This lack of concern suggests an adjustment to the status quo which, as Schein (1968) points out, can hardly be of ultimate benefit to the organisation. Growth and change require a creative tension between the worker and the organisation. What seems to happen in these institutions is a kind of 'burning out' of the enthusiasm, new ideas, and involvement that new staff bring to their work. The longer he has been in the institution, the more powerless and the less concerned about improvements a worker tends to feel.

Naturally, there are several ways of interpreting these associations between attitudes and length of service. Other studies of institutions for the retarded have noted such trends, but have interpreted them as an indication that staff members with certain kinds of backgrounds and personality features, especially those high in 'authoritarianism', tend to remain in these settings while less authoritarian workers tend to leave (Cleland & Peck, 1959; Williams, 1967). This can be termed a selection hypothesis, and it would tend to produce attitudinal differences of the sort we found when comparing short *v*. longer-service staff at any particular moment in time. An equally plausible interpretation, however, is that the experiences of work in these institutions can have a direct impact on a worker's feelings and attitudes (Porter, Lawler & Hackman, 1975). It seems perfectly likely that 'institutionalisation' as a social process applies to staff as well as inmates (see Goffman, 1961). Only a longitudinal study of staff attitudes over the course of their institutional careers could choose between these two interpretations of the exact processes involved in this effect—a study which would, it seems, be of great value to our understanding of these total institutions. Perhaps, as seems likely, both of these processes—selection and 'burning-out'—are involved.

Regardless of this question of interpretation, however, the attitude differentials found in our study between short- and long-service staff are not an encouraging commentary for residential facilities. On either interpretation, the setting has failed to sustain the input of a critically needed resource, the ideas (and perhaps the idealism) of new perspectives on the organisation and its provision of care. Instead, our evidence suggests that the institutional setting drains incoming staff of interest and energy, and then discards them, in one fashion or another.

As we showed above, care-taking by longer-service staff tends to be less stimulating, consistent with these attitude differences and our institutionalisation model. It is important to note here that these attitude and performance differences are unrelated to the *age* of the employee, or to any other personal background factor we could identify: younger attendants (those under the age of 30) show this pattern as clearly as do older workers. What may be crucial here is that the institutional settings we studied do not seem to provide the support or encouragement to direct-care workers to sustain their initial enthusiasm. This is a kind of wastefulness of resources seldom documented, but none the less unfortunate for all involved.

The impact of this process of disillusionment and increasing feelings of powerlessness is all the more striking when we compare the individual speech behaviour of attendants and their supervisors: with equivalent lengths of service, supervisors were significantly more likely to provide individualised care than were attendants. This strongly suggests the need for a promotional system that allows those who remain in service to find a means to maintain their sense of participation in the decision-making process and control over their own work life. A number of the workers wrote comments on their questionnaires to the effect that merit and effort were not appropriately rewarded in current promotional policy. Perhaps it is the frustration of an inadequate or even negative promotional and reward system that partly accounts for the less therapeutic attitudes and behaviour of long-stay subordinate staff. At any rate, attention to this institutionalisation of staff, and attempts to remedy it, seem imperative if we are to improve the quality of caretaking in these residential facilities.

Summary

We have just reviewed a large number of characteristics of the direct-care staff and their relationship to the care the residents receive. Attitudes and feelings of front-line workers have been argued to be of importance in understanding their job performance (Bogdan *et al.*, 1974; Aiken & Hage, 1966; Dailey, Allen, Chinsky & Veit, 1974, for example). We have found that the most powerful and consistent predictor of actual performance of these staff—that is, their interaction with the residents—is the extent to which they perceive themselves involved in matters relating to their work. This feeling of involvement appears to decrease when staff have been working in their buildings for more than one year. Staff with this length of service behind them are also staff who speak to the residents, if they do so at all, in a controlling rather than informative manner. Communication on a weekly basis with unit directors also appears to influence in a positive way those aspects of care which are subsumed in the RRMP. Since these are matters relating to daily routine, about which policy could be determined on a building basis, it would seem advisable for these staff to meet regularly with the individuals responsible for formulating such policy. Although our evidence does not suggest that increased frequency of meeting with such personnel by the direct-care staff influences their sense of involvement in decision making, it would seem to permit their involvement in discussion about matters relating to the residents' programmes and routines.

Age and sex of these staff are not consistently factors which influence the care they provide. We would not therefore see changes in hiring policies which discriminated in selection procedures on these criteria as solutions to the problems of providing improved care. We in fact concur with McLain and his colleagues (1974), who said, having used a measure similar to the RRMP with which to compare care practices within one institution, 'the effects of staff characteristics (age and sex) upon questionnaire scores are minimal' (p. 26).

The one demographic characteristic of staff which does appear to have a consistent effect on care (a negative one) is staff length of service. We have argued that this effect is a derivative of the process of disenchantment and discouragement we termed 'staff institutionalisation'—a process which may be endemic to such facilities to a degree, but also one which might be partially combated by more effective promotional policies within the institution. Cleland and Peck's work (1959) suggests that those direct-care staff who had long tenure in institutions were significantly more authoritarian, measured by the F scale, than those who left. As Butterfield (1968) has commented, if the 'successful' attendant is one who stays, the attributes which characterise him may not be the most desirable. We did not study the personalities of our direct-care staff but we have clear evidence that those who remained for more than a year were more institutionally oriented in their care-taking practices than those who had worked in these settings for a shorter period. Clearly the performance of direct-care staff who continue to work in an institution depends in part upon the characteristics of the person when hired and the relationship between these characteristics and the demands of the job. Administrative policies relating to selection and organisation could contribute to the reduction of staff institutionalisation.

Staff who are long-service members of the work force have been exposed far longer than their shorter-service colleagues to the practices and constraints of the institution. All these staff are at the bottom of the several hierarchies which exist in these facilities. It would not therefore be surprising if their performance and their perceptions of the organisations' structure were influenced by the behaviour of their superiors. We therefore want to consider the contribution of the supervisory staff to the care provided, and to shaping the organisational context in which direct-care staff work. From these considerations we may be able better to understand how the direct-care staff come to relate to the residents in the way they do. We turn in the next chapter to consider the organisaational factors operating on the direct-care staff's immediate superiors, namely the building heads.

12 THE BUILDING HEADS

We have just seen that some of the direct-care workers' perceptions of
the organisations they work in are linked to the variations in care they
provide. In Chapter 6 we described some of the characteristics of the
direct-care staff's immediate supervisors, the building heads. In this
chapter we want to examine the relationship between the characteristics of the building heads or supervisors – their reports of their involvement in decision making and their contact with other staff – and our
two indices of care-taking. We shall then examine the extent to which
care-taking tasks are specialised within these settings, and the ways in
which building heads might provide a model for their subordinates. We
will see what implications these factors have for the care provided for
the residents and we shall explore how the perceptions of the building
heads relate to their subordinates' perspectives, which in turn are linked
to variations in care.

Building Supervisors' Perceptions of Organisation and Care

Tizard *et al.* (1975) have argued that the freedom of a building head 'to
make decisions about matters which in other organisations are decided
centrally' (p. 8) is characteristic of what they term an autonomous unit.
Autonomy at this level, they argue, is 'a necessary condition for the performance of certain staff roles' (p. 10). We begin our examination of the building
supervisors in our study by examining the extent of their autonomy – in our
terms their perception of the degree of centralisation of authority.

To obtain their perceptions of the extent to which they were involved in
decision making as it related directly to the care of the residents and the
deployment of the direct-care staff we asked the building supervisors
eleven questions about matters relating to these areas. Specifically, they
were asked about the following matters: times residents awake in the
morning and retire at night; admission and discharge of residents; the
planning of residents' activities and home leave; the hiring and firing of
the direct-care staff; arrangements for days off and vacations for the
direct-care staff; and the planning of programmes for residents. They
indicated if they made decisions about these matters themselves, occasionally consulted with their superiors, regularly discussed matters with
them or were never consulted about these issues. It was from their responses to these questions that we developed an index of centralisation

Table 12.1: Distribution of Scores on Index of Centralisation

Building No.	Score
1	45.5
2	87.9
3	36.4
4	39.4
5	54.5
6	45.5
7	21.2
8	51.5
9	60.6
10	63.6
11	30.3
12	60.6
14	30.3
15	75.8
16	51.5
17	30.3
18	–
19	87.9
20	93.9
21	90.9

which we described in Chapter 4. Scores on this index could range from zero to 100 per cent, the high score representing maximum centralisation — i.e. no involvement by building supervisors in decision making. The scores on this index are given in Table 12.1 and as can be seen the scores vary markedly between the residences.

[In Building 18 there was no one formally assigned to the civil service posts which we have subsumed under the term building supervisor and it is therefore excluded from this part of the analysis.]

The mean score for the 20 buildings was 55.7, with a standard deviation of 22.7. Some indication of what these scores mean in terms of the building supervisors' participation in decision making can be gained by considering their involvement in each of the areas. Over half the building heads were regularly consulted or themselves made decisions about the time the residents went to bed (71 per cent); the placement of residents in activities (52 per cent); home leave for the residents (57 per cent); days off for direct-care staff (71 per cent) and holidays (81 per cent). It should be recalled that these residences were within institutions of the same types, all of which had undergone the same administrative met-amorphosis, i.e. had been unitised. The unit directors apparently involved the building heads to different degrees in terms of the issues to be decided on, for, in contrast to the above, two thirds of the building heads were not involved at all in the admission of residents or the hiring of staff to work in the buildings of which they were 'in charge'. Similarly 43 per cent of the building supervisors replied that they were never consulted about the firing of direct-care staff and 29 per cent said this was the case when residents were to be discharged.

Clearly these reported differences in participation in decision making, summarised in the index, suggest that in some buildings the people in daily charge felt considerable involvement in deciding resident care and staff allocation. In other buildings quite the opposite was felt by staff formally occupying the same civil service grade and the same position in the formal organisation's structure as far as any organisation chart would indicate. The charts we saw indeed indicated that all people in this position were of equal status. They may have been, but they were clearly different in terms of the authority they believed that they had.

The differences in the degree of centralisation reported were related to differences in the care of the residents as measured by the RRMP, ($r_{partial}$ = +.44, p<.05). They were not, however, related to differences in ISI scores. The former finding confirms that of King (1971) and his colleagues, but the absence of any significant relationship between the degree of centralisation and the type of language used by staff in the building in their interactions with residents points out the danger of assessing only one aspect of care when studying the effects of organ-isational factors. It appears that to increase the amount of informative speech in a building it is not enough merely to increase the extent to which a building head feels involved in decision making. This sense of involvement must extend to the subordinate care-taking staff as well — as we showed in the previous chapter. It seems reasonable that the build-ing supervisor's views should relate most directly to residence-wide policies, such as the RRMP measures, rather than to individual styles of care-taking as measured by the ISI.

We now turn to a consideration of the levels of communication these building heads experienced with three groups of colleagues — the profes-sionals, the unit directors, and the direct-care staff of other shifts. In Table 12.2 we present the scores on the index of communication with

Table 12.2: Distribution of Scores on Index of Communication with
          Professionals

Building No.	Score
1	16
2	14
3	13
4	16
5	13
6	14
7	10
8	16
9	16
10	11
11	17
12	14
14	18
15	15
16	18
17	20
18	–
19	14
20	19
21	23

professionals, and in Table 12.3 the scores on the indices of contact with
other shifts and the unit directors. The construction of these measures
is described in Chapter 4. The first measure represents the frequency
with which the building supervisors met with members of eight professional groups, physicians, registered nurses, psychologists, social workers,
teachers, occupational and physical therapists and rehabilitation council-
lors. In the majority of buildings, the contact the building supervisors
had with representatives of these professional services existing within
the institutions to provide a service for the residents was infrequent —
less often than once a week for more than two thirds of them as far as
teachers, occupational and physical therapists, and rehabilitation council-
lors were concerned. Ninety per cent of the building supervisors saw a
doctor at least weekly and 65 per cent saw a psychologist as often as
this. Nurses were seen as often as this by only 45 per cent of the building supervisors, and social workers by even fewer, 35 per cent.

Scores on the index in Table 12.2 could in theory range from eight, implying no contact at all with any of the personnel from these services, to 32, meaning daily contact with personnel from each group. The mean for the 20 buildings was 15.6, which reflects the overall low frequency with which these contacts occurred. The standard deviation (3.1) of this distribution suggests that there was relatively little variance between the residences in this low level of contact as well. Given this, it is perhaps not surprising that we found no correlation between scores on this index and scores on the ISI ($r_{partial}$ = .06). We did, however, find that scores on this index were inversely related at a significant level to scores on the RRMP ($r_{partial}$ = .50, p<.05). At face value this finding implies that the more frequent the contact the building heads have with these professionals, the more institution-oriented is the care provided in the building. This correlation, as usual, is open to a number of interpretations. It is not implausible that buildings known to be lacking in resources are being assigned professional staff in the hope that their input will improve the situation. In addition, it may well be that what is important is not the frequency of contact, but the content of this communication between professionals and building supervisors, which we made no attempt to study. This finding certainly suggests, however, that merely increasing the availability of professional resources to building heads will *not* improve those aspects of care measured by the RRMP in any dramatic and rapid fashion (and possibly may even inhibit such improvement). Perhaps professionals from the backgrounds we found available in these settings were not people with the appropriate skills to improve the quality of care in these buildings. As Butterfield (1968) has commented, 'professionals can be intolerant of problems with which attendants must cope' (p. 324).

Table 12.3 shows clearly that there were differences between the buildings in the extent to which the building supervisors were in contact with the unit directors and colleagues on other shifts.

The variance on these communication measures is greater than that for professional contact, and over all the average level of contact is higher. These scores represent the frequency with which the meetings occurred directly since a score of four was given where contact occurred daily, a score of three where it occurred weekly, and two and one where it occurred monthly or less often, respectively. The mean score on contact with the unit directors was 3.36 (standard deviation = 0.89), indicating that, over all, building heads and unit directors meet at least weekly. There is more variation in the frequency with which building supervisors attend inter-shift meetings, the mean for the group being 4.1 and the standard

Table 12.3: Distribution of Scores on Index of Frequency of Contact
with Unit Directors and Co-workers

Building No.	Index of contact with unit directors	Index of contact with co-workers
1	4	1
2	4	3
3	4	3
4	3	4
5	4	3
6	3	3
7	3	3
8	3	3
9	4	2
10	4	4
11	4	3
12	4	3
14	3	4
15	4	2
16	4	1
17	4	2
18	—	—
19	2	2
20	1	1
21	2	1

deviation 7.07. In three buildings, for example, such meetings occur daily, and in nine they occur once a week. In other buildings they are less frequent occurrences.

Frequent meetings with the unit directors does appear to have positive consequences for care as measured by the RRMP ($r_{partial}$, -.40, p<.05), as does more frequent contact between the shifts ($r_{partial}$, -.48, p<.05). However, a higher frequency of contact between the building supervisors and both these groups does not appear significantly related to the care being provided as it is measured by the ISI. Frequent contact between the unit directors and the building supervisors would permit discussion of a daily programme to implement resident-oriented care, as well as a review of the problems and progress staff experience in doing this. Similarly, frequent meetings between the shifts would encourage continuity of such programming and reduce inconsistencies simply because the staff have a chance to discuss plans for the residents. Again, however, we have evidence that suggests that not all aspects of care are equally affected by specific dimensions of the organisation's structure. Treatment practices, as policies characterising the residence, seem to be related to the building head's perspective. Actual talk between the staff and residents may be more likely to be affected by behaviour and practices which the direct-care staff can see. Perhaps this is an area of care which is most likely to be immediately influenced by the style of the building head. There is some evidence for this argument in the data we obtained to study the degree of specialisation of task in the residences between subordinates and the building heads.

Role Specialisation and Care

The method of collecting data on staff roles and specialisation of task has been described in Chapter 4. It will be recalled that we classified our observations of staff activities into six categories, three of which subsumed activities directly involving staff with the residents. These three categories were: functional care, such as washing and dressing the residents; social care, such as playing games with or chatting with residents; and supervisory care accompanied by speech or physical contact with the resident, such as conversing with a resident while supervising his meal. The other activities did not intrinsically involve staff with residents. These were: domestic activities, such as washing floors; administrative activities, such as filling out forms; and a sixth category, miscellaneous, which we used for activities which could not be subsumed under any of the five types, like walking from one room to another.

Building supervisors and attendants were observed for two morning and two afternoon shifts. No observations of the building head were made on the afternoon shift in Building 14, and there were only attendants in Building 18 during our observations there so that data on building supervisors' activities could not be compiled for these two buildings. The frequency of those activities which directly involve the staff with the residents are compared with those activities which did not involve them with the residents—domestic care and administrative activities in Tables 12.4 and 12.5.

As can be seen from Table 12.4, there is an extremely wide range— from 10.5 per cent to 69.8 per cent—in the extent to which building supervisors in these residences are involved in activities which directly concern the residents. The overall mean for this staff group in terms of these activities is 46 per cent. When we examined the relationship

Table 12.4: Proportion of Building Heads' roles comprised of Functional,
Social and Supervisory Care involving Interaction with Residents

Building No.	Proportion of Functional, Social and Supervisory activities
1	45.2
2	30.6
3	42.6
4	62.4
5	43.0
6	40.3
7	51.9
8	56.1
9	35.9
10	69.8
11	10.5
12	55.6
13	43.3
14	–
15	63.8
16	39.4
17	24.2
18	–
19	39.2
20	67.6
21	59.0

between the extent of functional, social and supervisory activity by the
building heads and our outcome measures, we found that the extent of
involvement in these activities is not significantly related to care practices
as measured in the RRMP Scale. However, as predicted, the proportion
of informative speech is strongly related to the percentage of high
frequency of these kinds of activities in the supervisor's role ($r_{partial}$ =
.73, p<.01).

When we look at Table 12.5, we see that there is a similarly wide range
in the proportion of activities building heads were engaged in which were
domestic and administrative in nature, ranging from 32.4 per cent to
79.4 per cent, with an overall mean of 58 per cent.

Examining the relationship of this index to our outcome measures,
we found that there was a significant negative correlation with inform-

Table 12.5: Proportion of Building Heads' Role comprised of Domestic and Administrative Activities

Building No.	Proportion of domestic and administrative activities
1	68.9
2	54.4
3	32.4
4	55.2
5	49.3
6	73.6
7	51.1
8	44.6
9	73.4
10	58.2
11	52.3
12	79.4
13	77.8
14	—
15	40.0
16	55.6
17	69.6
18	—
19	67.6
20	51.0
21	46.2

ative speech ($r = -.42$, $p < .05$). Thus buildings where the supervisors are more fully engaged in domestic and administrative activities tend to be characterised by less informative speech. We found a weaker non-significant trend in the same direction with scores on the RRMP Scale ($r = +.29$).

To test our hypothesis about the effects of specialisation on care provided, we constructed an index of specialisation of the frequency of observed types of activity between the two status groups within the building. We have described the procedure used to do this in Chapter 4. The higher the score the greater the specialisation of role activities between the two status groups. Table 12.6 shows the distribution of scores on this specialisation index for each building.

Building 14 was again excluded from this analysis, but Building 18 is

Table 12.6: Distribution of Scores on Index of Specialisation

Building No.	Score
1	53.5
2	109.6
3	71.0
4	19.7
5	43.0
6	77.4
7	52.6
8	78.6
9	57.8
10	58.3
11	95.8
12	73.6
13	30.6
14	–
15	53.6
16	73.0
17	139.3
18	0.0
19	35.1
20	31.7
21	37.6

scored as zero of necessity, since only attendants work in this building and no specialisation along status group lines is therefore possible. This role specialisation measure is correlated with the ability level of the residents ($r = -.47$, p is $<.05$, two-tailed). In lower ability buildings, roles tend towards more specialisation. We found that the quality of care as measured by the RRMP Scale is not related to role specialisation between the building staff status groups ($r_{partial} = +.32$). However, role specialisation is related to the amount of informative language used by building staff ($r_{partial} = -.40$, p$<.05$). This finding indicates that greater role specialisation between building staff status groups has a detrimental effect on the quality of care as measured by the ISI. Conversely, in buildings where both staff groups do very similar amounts of the various tasks which have to be done, it appears that care is more resident-oriented, at least in so far as the speech of the staff is concerned.

The proportion of administrative activity carried out by the heads of the buildings was closely related to the degree of specialisation character-ising the building ($r = +.75$, $p < .01$). Reciprocally, the proportion of activities carried out by the heads of the buildings which directly involve them with the residents was strongly negatively related to the degree of role specialisation in the buildings ($r = -.62$, $p < .01$).

This pattern of findings indicated that where building heads' roles contain a higher proportion of activities which do not directly involve them with the residents, this may limit the possibility of their providing a role model for care-taking. These data provide support for our suggestion that the characteristic style of a daily activity, like speech, is more likely to be influenced by direct example than by differences in the wider structural properties of the organisation.

Relationships Between Supervisors' and Subordinates' Views

If, as we have argued, it is important empirically to distinguish and measure different dimensions of an organisation's structure, it is surely important to understand the relationships between the parts of that structure. As we begin to do this, we can gradually start to understand how differences operating at one level of a hierarchy may have signif-icance for the differences we have observed at other levels. We now turn to trying to do this within the organisation of the residence itself, by looking at the interrelationship of the organisational characteristics operating at the building head and direct-care staff levels.

Let us describe first a simple model which we developed on the basis of the data we have described in this chapter and the last. Buildings in which building heads reported that they are involved in decision making are likely to be ones in which they are also involved in discussions with unit directors about policy matters relating to the daily management of the residents, and in consequence ones in which they would be meeting with other shift members to communicate about such matters and ensure continuity of practice. In such buildings, the direct staff would clearly meet with other shift members and feel more involved in decision making as well. This greater sense of involvement, the possibility of dis-cussing problems of implementing policy with colleagues and of passing on to them and obtaining from them information about the residents, should ultimately lead to more resident-oriented care practices and a higher level of morale.

At the direct-care staff level, higher centralisation (low levels of per-ceived participation in decision making) is related to low staff morale. The degree of centralisation at this staff level is not related to specialisation, nor to any of the measures of communication, but greater decentralisation is inversely related to higher levels of formalisation. Formalisation is not related to either specialisation or communication levels, however. Where there is little participation in decision making and the division of labour is specialised along status lines, staff will have a low morale level since there is little room left for initiative or diversity in role performance. A high level of specialisation is related to low morale amongst direct-care staff ($r = -.49$, $p < .05$). We can express all this positively by stating that where decentralisation is high and formalisation is low, there is more room for initiative and flexibility in the carrying out of tasks, and where this is reinforced by low levels of specialisation in the division of labour along status lines, staff morale is positively reinforced since their job content is more varied. A low level of specialisation also provides direct-care staff with direct models which are likely to influence, as we have indeed suggested they do, the way in which they interact with the residents.

Figure 1 shows the relationships between the organisational variables we actually found to exist within these two staffing levels in the caretaking hierarchy and between them.

The interrelations of the two organisational levels can be briefly summarised. Only two of the supervisor factors are associated with important direct-care variables: building meetings and professional contacts. These two factors are inversely related to each other, and they are also oppositely related to perceived involvement in decision making by the subordinate building staff: *more* professional contact and *fewer* building meetings are associated with lower feelings of involvement. Continuing this reciprocal pattern, more professional contact is also associated with high levels of formalisation (a variable with an inhibitory relation to the ISI, it will be recalled), while more frequent building meetings appear to improve staff morale. All in all, Figure 1 suggests rather consistently a 'positive' cluster of supervisor factors — especially frequent building meetings and more unit director contact — which facilitate direct-care staff perspectives that have a positive effect on care. In sharp contrast, frequent professional contacts, at least as measured in our particular fashion, appear to inhibit these same positive direct-care staff variables. The implication here is not that all professional support to these residential facilities needs to be removed, but it seems ill advised simply to assume that more frequent contact, regardless of how structured, between building staff and the professional departments will prove helpful. Our results surely highlight the need to question this usually implicit assumption thoroughly. On the other hand, they do suggest that some of the residences with high levels of unit director input may obtain some of the effects originally anticipated for

Figure 1: Significant Relationships Among Important Organisational
        Factors Measured at Two Levels

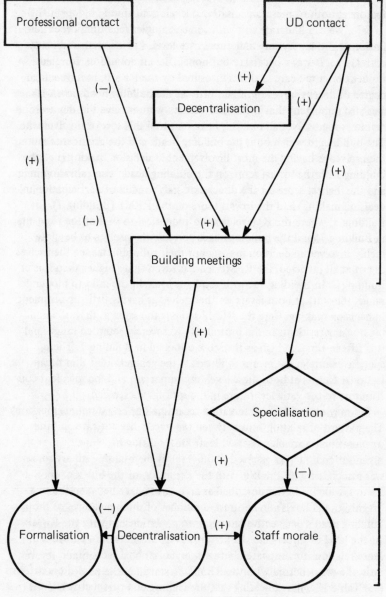

*p's < .10; signs in ( ) indicate direction of relationships;

factors measured by Building head interview in ▭

factors measured by direct-care worker questionnaire in ◯

the process of unitisation itself. It is important to keep in mind that
factors at both of these organisational levels contributed independently
to care. We can illustrate this with some examples regarding decentralisation at the supervisory and direct-care levels (which are not directly
correlated). It was a necessary but not sufficient condition, to effect
resident-oriented care as this is measured by the RRMP, to have a high
degree of decentralisation of authority at the building heads level. It
was also important that their sudordinates were involved in the decision-
making process. Not all building heads ensured this sort of involvement.
The building in which both the building heads *and* the attendants saw
themselves as having the most involvement in decision making (i.e., the
building with the lowest score on the building heads' centralisation index,
and the highest score on the direct-care staff's index of participation in
decision making) had the lowest score on the RRMP (Building 7). In
Building 3, where the IQ level is almost identical to that of the residents
in Building 7, and the building heads perceive themselves to be quite
highly involved in decision making but their subordinates see themselves
as not at all involved, the RRMP score is seven times higher than it is in
Building 7. In Building 21, with residents again in the mild to moderate
range, the staff at both levels see themselves as having little involvement
in decision making. Here the RRMP score is the same as that of a building housing residents in the profoundly to severely retarded range, and
it is fifteen times as high as the score obtained in Building 7. These
specific examples are meant to illustrate the general point that organisational factors at both these levels are important and independent contributors to the variance in care in the settings we studied.

We may end with an observation regarding our two outcome measures.
The pattern of relationships between the two indices of care and the
organisational variables assessed is strikingly different. None of the
organisational factors assessed at the level of the building supervisors
was associated with the ISI (with the exception of the index of specialisation, which is better described as an intermediary between the two
organisational levels). In contrast, a number of these measures of the
building head's perspective entered into a relationship with the RRMP.
At the level of direct-care worker, however, this pattern was reversed.
More relationships appeared between organisational factors and the ISI;
rather fewer occurred with the RRMP. We might summarise these patterns
(see Table 12.7) as indicating that the feelings and perspectives of the
building supervisors appear more important predictors of the system of
residence-wide treatment practices (as indexed by the RRMP), while the
feelings and reactions of the direct-care workers appear more related to

The Building Heads

137

Table 12.7: Summary of Significant Relations Between Two Outcome Measures and Level of Assessment for Organisational Variable

		ISI	RRMP
Building Head's Perspective	Centralisation	–	*
	Communication w/ professionals	–	*
	Communication w/ unit directors	–	*
	Inter-shift building meetings	–	*
Direct-Care Worker's Perspective	Role Specialisation	*	–
	Centralisation	*	*
	Formalisation	*	–
	Communication w/ professionals	*	–
	Communication w/ unit directors	–	*
	Inter-shift building meetings	–	–
	Staff morale (Co-worker helpfulness)	*	–

* $p < .05$, one-tailed.

the detailed style of staff/resident interaction (as indexed by the ISI). These two patterns seem reasonable: the typical treatment practices of a residence should be more under the discretionary control of the supervisor than should the details of actual staff/resident interaction. More than anything else, however, these results highlight again the need to consider a variety of dimensions of care and a breadth of organisational perspectives when investigating complex organisations of this sort.

Summary

The policy implications of this chapter may be briefly summarised. To improve care we suggest that a two-pronged approach is necessary. To ensure high standards in the management of daily events the building heads have to have a high level of involvement in decisions about the residents and in turn they must involve their staff in these decisions. This has to be linked with frequent meetings between them, staff in the buildings, and the unit directors. To ensure improvements in the frequency with which staff speak to residents informatively, a low level of specialisation is necessary in the division of labour between building heads and direct-care staff, a perception of some freedom from rigid constraints must be established, *and* methods to increase the direct-care staffs' participation in decision making must be developed. We have observed differences among the building heads in the perception of their role. We now know that these are related to specific aspects of the residents' care, and have implications, as does the extent to which they specialise their role, for the behaviour of their direct-care staff. In the next chapter, we examine some of the possible reasons for the observed differences in the structural characteristics of the building supervisors' role within these institutional settings.

13 ADMINISTRATIVE STAFF

The direct-care staff and the building supervisors affect the daily management of the residents. We described in Chapter 8 the variety of ways in which they carry out their care-taking activities. In the last two chapters we discussed some of the organisational characteristics of the residences, the immediate work situation of these two groups of staff, as well as some of their personal characteristics. We have seen how these are related to the variations in care practice. We have argued that aspects of the organisational structure of the residences are important contributors to the quality of care provided in them. However, these residences and the staff who work in them do not exist in a vacuum. We have already noted that, in their work, residence staff come into contact with other personnel in the institutions, the professionals and unit directors whose primary work location is not in the residences. The activities of these people, along with those of the superintendents and department heads, will in part define the work situation of the care staff. In this chapter we want to consider some of the ways in which features of the wider organisational context of the institution could act as enabling or inhibiting constraints upon the organisation of the residences.

We start by considering the position of the immediate superiors of the staff who provide daily care for the residents, namely the unit directors. We examine in particular the extent of their authority. We then discuss some of the views of the chief executives of these settings, the superintendents, and finally indicate ways in which the administrative staff in these institutions may influence the work situation of the care-takers and through this their care-taking activity. To do this we draw on data collected in interviews with unit directors, department heads and superintendents of the three institutions. As we noted in Chapter 4, our data from these sources are essentially descriptive and far less detailed than those which we collected on the residences. We nevertheless think it is important to present them because the residences are part of larger complex institutions. By using these descriptive data we may gain some insight into the way the wider institution impinges upon the organisation of the residences.

All these institutions, from which we selected the residences we have described, had been unitised, as we noted in Chapter 1. In theory this meant 'a revolution of the administrative structure. Its most important feature is that the School will be subdivided into smaller functional units, each of which will be headed by a director with a considerable degree of authority and responsibility' (Farrell & Moser, 1969). These institutions were certainly subdivided into units and each unit had its director. The responsibilities of the unit directors are clearly stated in the civil service job description for the position. They were to 'direct a functional unit with particular responsibility for the design, development and implement- ation of services appropriate to the unit's residents and day trainees' (Commonwealth of Massachusetts, 1969). They were also to 'direct the unit's team' and supervise 'all personnel assigned to a functional unit'. The numbers of residents for whom the nine unit directors we inter- viewed were thus responsible varied *within* and *between* the institutions, as Table 13.1 indicates.

Table 13.1: Unit Size: Buildings and Number of Residents in Nine Units Surveyed

	Unit	Number of Buildings	Number of Residents
Institution A	1	3	181
	2	5	290
	3	2	82
	4	2	101
Institution B	5	4	187
	6	4	309
	7	2	120
Institution C	8	6	124
	9	5	431

The size of these units is clearly variable, ranging from one with 82 res- idents to one with 431. As far as the numbers of residents for whom programmes had to be designed and in terms of the formal job description, the unit directors' responsibilities were indeed considerable.

The unit directors had to seek assistance from a wide variety of person- nel in the institution to obtain resources for the development and implementation of services and programmes for residents. One group of these were the department heads. In the formal organisation chart, which reflected the civil service grading of posts, the unit directors were assigned a grade considerably below the level of the department heads in terms both of salary and prestige. These people controlled many of the personnel and other resources required by the unit directors, and it is not surprising given their subordinate status that all the unit directors reported difficulty in obtaining the assistance of these department heads in the implementation of activities for their units. To carry out their duties would require, amongst other things, that the unit directors have authority to create a team of professional personnel.

The Unit Team and Professional Services

In theory, the basic unit team, in so far as professional services were concerned, was meant to consist of a nurse, a physician, a social worker, a psychologist, and the unit director. Speech and hearing services, as well as education, rehabilitation, and physical and occupational therapy, were to be available as necessary. Not all of the departments had enough staff to assign one person to work full-time with each unit. The decision as to how these professional staff should be deployed in relation to the units was left in practice to the department heads.

Of the four professional departments with staff to make up the basic unit team, not one operated with any formal written description of their relationship to the units. At Institution B physicians were assigned to units; however, none of the physicians at Institutions A and C were thus assigned. In these two institutions a physician could work in residences which were in different units, and each unit director would therefore have to relate to several members of this department. Nurses, like physicians, were also to be found working in every building, but in Institution B they were 'loaned' to the buildings. By contrast, in the other two settings these staff were assigned on a unit basis. All the social workers were assigned to units, but shortage of staff meant that two of the four units studied at Institution A were without social workers, as was one of those at Institution B. All the psychologists were assigned on a unit basis, but one unit each at Institutions A and B was without this professional input, because of staff shortages in the psychology departments. Over all, then, six of the nine units had complete unit teams. The size of the unit and functional level of its residents was unrelated to the assignment of these four professional services to the unit. Unit directors were rarely consulted about the assignment of particular personnel from these professional departments. Once they had arrived and become part of the unit directors' team, the unit directors' reports to us about the accountability of these staff for their work presented a confused picture. In five units (3, 4, 5, 6 and 7) the unit directors said they had no authority to determine what any of these staff would do. By way of contrast, in three units (1, 2 and 6) all professional staff were seen as directly answerable to the unit directors for their work. In one unit the unit director reported that the social workers, but *not* the physicians, the nurses, or the psychologists, were accountable to him.

There was also some lack of consensus in the opinions of the department heads and the unit directors involved, as to who had control over the work of the professionals assigned to the unit team and when and where they would carry out their work. Only at Institution B were the unit directors and the heads of the medical and nursing services agreed that authority for the work of the physicians and nurses was exclusively a matter for the directors of these two services. At both Institutions A and C, some of the unit directors disagreed with the assessment of the department heads of these services regarding their control over these members of the unit team.

Potential sources of conflict also existed between the unit directors and the directors of psychology and social work. At Institution A the head of the department of social work said that authority had been delegated to the unit directors. Two of the four unit directors we interviewed there, however, thought that the director of social work still retained control over the social workers assigned to the unit teams. By contrast the unit directors at Institution B thought they had control over the activities of the social workers assigned to them but the department head there said that she had not delegated the authority to them. Only at Institution C was everyone involved in agreement that the unit directors were accountable for the work of the social workers in their unit team. A similar situation existed *vis-à-vis* the psychology service in the three settings.

None of the institutions had gone as far as that described by Kiger (1966) or Henninger (1963). In both of these, the dual accountability of professional personnel to department heads and unit directors produced so much conflict that departments as such were disbanded, the department heads themselves were assigned to units and retained administrative responsibility only for recruitment and liaison with external professional bodies.

Two thirds of the unit directors in the three institutions clearly did not see themselves as having any control over the activities of professionals in the unit teams. Additionally there is evidence of conflict, actual and potential, between the unit directors in all three institutions and both the heads of departments and professional staff assigned to units. Our interviews with the unit directors suggested that the constraints upon their authority were not limited to those imposed by the heads of the professional departments.

All equipment and building services like linen, crockery, furniture and residents' clothing have to be requisitioned from a central supply department in these institutions. Thus unit directors have to negotiate with the directors of the hotel service departments for these. They have no budget for their units since funding from the state legislature was provided on an institution-wide basis. The unit directors inevitably competed with each other for scarce resources, one of which was direct-care staff. They had no control over the numbers of these personnel assigned to their unit. All but one of the unit directors reported that control over staffing numbers to the three shifts working in the residences was in the hands of either an assistant superintendent, the director of personnel or the director of the nursing service. The extent of their control over the acquisition of equipment, professional and other services necessary to run the units as well as the numbers of direct-care staff to work in them was clearly very limited. Their authority within the residences was thus clearly constrained by the activities of other members of the institutions. Yet it was the unit directors who were formally charged with planning and developing programmes for the residents.

Unit Directors' Authority within the Residences

As a group the unit directors did not perceive themselves to have much authority *vis-à-vis* the residences in their unit. In Table 13.2 we summarise the responses of the unit directors to our questions about their participation in decisions relating to the staff who worked in their units and the activities that went on there.

Clearly it is only in three areas — planning programmes for residents, arranging their home leave or a transfer to another unit — that all the unit directors see themselves as having authority to make decisions. In all other areas relating to the residents' activities there is little consensus about their authority, except in determining meal times. Most of the unit directors expressed frustration at not being able to change the times, which were controlled by the central kitchen and the operation of the food trucks which delivered meals to the residences in the units. Those unit directors who felt they had no control over the timing of other daily activities said they had been unable to change traditionally established practices. As far as the care staff working in their units are concerned most of the unit directors decided when they should take time off and what they should do whilst at work but there is no consensus about their control over the hiring of these staff and it is clear that a unit director is not given authority to dismiss a care staff member. In

Table 13.2: Unit Directors' Participation in Decisions Relating to Matters Within Their Units

Area	Participate in decision making	Do not participate in decision making
Hiring care staff	7	2
Firing care staff	0	9
Days off for care staff	6	3
Holidays for care staff	8	1
Daily tasks of care staff	8	1
Residents' programmes	9	0
Home leave for residents	9	0
Transfer of residents to other units	9	0
Admission of residents to units	4	5
Meal times for residents	1	8
Bed times for residents	7	2
Getting-up times for residents	6	3

practice, as we learnt from these directors and superintendents, all care staff are on probation for six months. After this period only the superintendent has legal authority to dismiss care staff. Unit directors could make recommendations for dismissal which might or might not be upheld by the superintendent. Given that, along with tenure after the six months' probationary period, also comes the right for care staff to appeal against any dismissal notice to the Civil Service Commission, it is not surprising that superintendents were loathe to support a recommendation to dismiss a member of the care staff.

The unit directors' formally assigned responsibilities were considerable. Clearly this could not be said for the authority they were given to discharge their duties. There was often little consensus amongst them about the extent of their authority and much that they said indicated that it was severely limited. The nature of their authority is perhaps best summarised by one of their number and by one of the superintendents. The former said 'you can gain personal respect, but that doesn't get you mops; there comes a point where personal respect isn't enough'. The superintendent, perhaps more cynical, perhaps more realistic, than her colleagues, described the unit directors as being 'idealistic' and 'having no administrative experience'. She went on to say that 'At first they are buddy-buddy with the attendants and the unions. After one year they see how things are and then they're burnt out.' Few of them operated in practice as we have indicated, with either the resources they needed to do their job as it is described in the civil service codes, or with the formal authority to acquire these resources.

Implications of Constraints on Unit Director Authority

It is impossible to delegate authority unless you have it, though of course it does not necessarily follow that having leads to giving. The less you have, however, the less you can give. The unit directors did report to us that they sometimes delegated authority or involved building supervisors in decision making when it was possible to do so. One unit director, for example, reported that she had made the building supervisors entirely responsible for deciding when the building staff should have their days off. In two units, the administration of the building *within* the units was not consistent. The unit directors in Units 1 and 2 said they differentiated the extent to which they involved their various building heads in deciding when residents would do certain activities, and which direct-care staff would do which tasks. In Unit 1, the same discriminating strategy was used by the unit director in relation to determining days off for the building staff.

Because we had asked both groups of staff about decision making in some identical areas of activity we were able directly to examine the extent to which the unit directors and the building supervisors agreed that the latter were involved by the unit directors in making decisions in these areas. In seven of the ten cases in which the building heads saw themselves as highly involved in decision making, the unit directors said that they involved them to some degree in decision making in areas of activity about which we asked them both. There is then a little evidence that there was some consensus between the two groups about involvement in decision making. Our numbers are small and our measures crude (highly involved in decision making = below the mean on the building heads index and involvement of the building heads in eighty per cent of the same items as assessed by the unit directors).

In one sense this is a crude validation of our index of centralisation, developed from the responses of the building heads to our questions about their involvement in decision making. More substantially it suggests that where the unit directors do have authority and then permit their building heads to participate in decisions over which they have control, this may ultimately have positive consequences for the resident's care. As we have seen, involvement of the building heads in decision making (and ultimately, the extension of this involvement to direct-care workers) was related to resident-oriented care on the dimensions measured by the

RRMP and the ISI. The more involvement of building supervisors, the more resident-oriented is care on the RRMP, and when this is extended to the care-takers themselves, the higher are ISI scores as well. Only to the extent that the unit directors *have* authority, is it possible for them to involve their building heads in decision making. It is obvious that when they have no control over resources, staffing numbers, professional input in the same areas and aspects of the resident's daily life, they cannot delegate any authority in these areas to their building heads. We have made it clear that the unit directors can operate under many constraints, and in certain areas of their work they had no effective authority at all. Since the accounts they gave us of their authority varied within institutions as well as between them, it is hardly surprising that we observed variability in the building heads' perceptions of the extent to which they were involved in decision making.

The Superintendents

The superintendents of these three institutions were not without constraints on their own authority. They had to work with a number of diverse and competing factions within and outside the institutions. They administered complex organisations in which personnel with their own special interests, the unions, the unit directors, the department heads, vied for their support. In Institutions A and B the superintendents estimated they spent 95 per cent of their time on day-to-day problems, putting out fires of one kind or another. The superintendent in Institution C was only marginally better off in this respect, estimating that he spent 85 per cent of his time in this manner as compared to long-term planning. Their goals were varied and not consonant with those of their deputies. In one institution the superintendent wanted to blow the place up whilst her deputy was intent on pursuing activities to improve it. Groups from outside the institution were often vociferous in their demands on the superintendent. Such demands were often conflicting. Universities wanted better teaching facilities, parents wanted better care and state administrators wanted financial savings.

The legislature imposed constraints upon their authority too. Legally, the superintendents could not delegate their authority to dismiss staff to other personnel within the institution. The state had established a budget procedure which clearly imposed control over the superintendents' disbursement of funds which were allocated. All budget estimates are submitted 18 months in advance of their allocation. A budget was requested for the institution as a whole, not, as noted, made up on a unit basis. This was submitted to the regional office where it was assessed in terms of the region's priorities and trimmed or weighted accordingly. From there it was sent to the central Department of Mental Health, undergoing another review in the context of the overall departmental review. From there it went to the Department of Human Services, a state-wide agency acting as an umbrella for all human service departments in the state and from thence to the Department of Administration and Finance, and finally to the legislature, where the requested appropriations were voted upon. In terms of notification of the actual appropriation, one of the superintendents pointed out that they were preparing for the following year's budget before they knew what they had been allocated for the current fiscal year. The budgets were drawn up in terms of a series of accounts and money was not transferable from one account to another without formal application to the Bureau of Administration and Finance. According to one of the superintendents any expenditure under one of these account heads for more than 100 dollars had to be approved by the central department, which often meant that they lost items because of this delay, or that many items were purchased in 99 dollar lots.

It is not easy to purchase a van to transport the residents for 99 dollars, no matter how many lots one attempts to do this in. The superintendent at C told us that he had failed to acquire a van to ferry the residents in because the application sat on the desk of someone in the Bureau of Administration and Finance until the fiscal year ended. At that point, he was told that the requisition was no longer admissible because the fiscal year had ended. A new requisition would have to be made out, but since no application had been made for such an item in the new budget, he was advised that he was unlikely to get it.

The Superintendents and the Units

The superintendents all admitted that there were problems in the operation of the units. Two of them said that the relationship between the professional departments and the units was poor, and one of them said it was varied, being 'excellent' in the case of social work service, 'good' as far as the psychology and nursing departments were concerned, and 'questionable' as far as all the other professional departments were concerned. (Interestingly enough this was the institution in which the head of the department of social work and the unit directors agreed that authority to control the work of the social workers had been delegated to the unit directors.) The co-operation of the hotel service departments within the units was rated as poor by the superintendent in Institution C, 'in some cases poor and in others fair' by the superintendent of B, and as 'average' by the superintendent of A. The superintendent at B, commenting on these relationships, told us that she had ordered the steward to allocate his domestic staff to the units. He had done this and subsequently she heard complaints again about the cleanliness of the buildings. Upon further investigation, she discovered that the steward, while complying with her order which meant that he lost some of the staff in his 'empire', had simply discontinued the ordering of cleaning materials. The superintendents were equally lacking in enthusiasm about the relationship between their own offices and the unit directors. Their assessment of unitisation *per se* was varied, and by and large negative. One of them summarising the situation reflects their views. This superintendent said unitisation 'hadn't made tremendous or significant changes'; it had however 'increased the bickering amongst the kingdom builders'.

The unit directors were introduced into complex organisations. Little consideration was given to the way in which they would be integrated into such complex structures to enable them to carry out their formally assigned duties. It is not surprising, though perhaps saddening, that they then should be seen by the chief executive of these institutions to have contributed little to improving care, simply added to the competing factions demanding support and resources from the superintendents.

Summary

These institutions are clearly complex places, not in themselves isolated from the pressures of different interest groups in the communities surrounding them. However, as Tizard, Sinclair & Clarke (1975) pointed out, 'institutions differ in their permeability as in everything else, but their relative imperviousness permits their high level of diversity' (p. 7). Within these three institutions all providing care for the same type of client, the mentally handicapped, it is very clear that diversity exists. It characterises care-taking practices and dimensions of the organisational structure at every level and the attributes the personnel who work in them bring to their work. The superintendents and departmental directors impose limits on the autonomy of the unit directors. High-sounding policy statements of the senior administrators were hardly translated into organisational systems which would ensure the implementation of the goals outlined in those statements.

As far as we know, all the superintendents we interviewed are no longer working at the institutions. In A and B they retired, in C the superintendent resigned. The residents we knew are by and large still there; we have not been able to follow up the unit directors or department heads we interviewed.

One consistent feature of the process of unitisation, we have noted, is the potentially dangerous practice of grouping residents together in terms of the similarity of their functional abilities. This practice character- ised all three institutions, and our evidence suggests its costs for the least able. Even within a world of deprived and handicapped persons, the less you've got, the less you get in such places, where you are housed with others like yourself. Whether you get any more if you are less able living in the same residences as your more able peers remains to be seen.

One other consistent consequence of the appointment of unit directors was the feeling of frustration expressed by the unit directors themselves. They all worked hard and for long hours, yet there is little to show as a direct effect of their labours in the way of positive consequences for the institutions.

One of us (NVR) worked in Institution A prior to unitisation, and for another purpose collected data on the care provided for the residents in a number of buildings, using the RRMP. The scores on the buildings studied prior to unitisation were compared with the scores we obtained on this measure four years later, three years after the implementation of unitisation. In these same buildings we found that the mean score had dropped from 27.09 in 1969 to 23.9 in 1973. The change in scores, while indicating that over all the buildings had become a little more resident-oriented in their care, was not statistically significant. Nor was the direction of change consistent on this measure. Two of the buildings had become more institution-oriented over this time period. One had decreased its score by 20 points on this scale. We should note that there had been some changes in the composition of the resident population in some buildings, which we were not able to control for in the analysis. However, it is suggestive of the small rewards for the work of the unit director, or perhaps more accurately, unitisation as it was operating in those settings. Perhaps this is not surprising when we reflect on the limits that many of them felt were imposed on their attempts to implement change, and if they felt themselves powerless it is equally unsurprising that those who provided direct care for the residents thought, as one worker put it, that 'nobody listens to us'.

In one of the public statements describing the nature of unitisation, amongst the benefits of its implementation was to be improved com- munication. It was pointed out that under the system which was to be replaced by unitisation, the staffing assignments hardly ever overlapped, so that 'a physician may have building A, B, C, and the nursing super- visor building A, E, F, and the psychologist A, G, and H etc.' (Farrell & Moser, 1969). In some instances unitisation had begun to remedy this and create a situation in which it was possible for a group of professional staff to be jointly responsible for a single group of residents. In other situations this was clearly not the case. Whilst in some cases the short-fall was a product of staff shortages in the particular professional depart-ment, in others it reflected a failure on the part of the departmental heads to assign their staff on a unit basis, and the insistence of their superintendent that they should do so.

The unit directors' comments to us underline what we have reported here—the lack of clarity in their role, the low level of authority, and the poor communication between themselves and at least some of the service departments with which they had to negotiate. They had plenty to say spontaneously about these matters and, perhaps not surprisingly, their comments all had a similar ring. We quote from a number of them. Some had their own explanation for the communication problems between themselves and the departments. One, in the institution where the director of nursing said they loaned their staff to the units, made the following comment: 'Many of the nursing service have refused to work with the unit directors. If anyone in the nursing service does go along with the unit directors they are black-listed in the nursing service. The unit directors are a threat to the authority of the nursing service.' Another unit director at Institution C said, 'I would like to see the unit directors completely in charge, with all service people lined out to the Units. Dep-artment heads should function as consultants and should not have admin-istrative duties like arranging hours of work, days off etc.' They were also critical of the work of their professional colleagues. At Institution B, one of them said, 'I'd like to see realistic programmes implemented. Some of the programmes exist in terms of how the professionals see them, often they don't relate to the actual populations we have.' Another unit director said, 'It's essential to establish who is boss. We must improve communications between all areas. Unit directors have come and gone very fast, they all have different notions of the role. The biggest problem is communication between building staff and all other departments in-cluding the superintendents.' Two remarks made time and time again to us were 'there is no clear chain of command', and 'we lack authority to make decisions'. This lack of authority did not extend merely to their control over the work of the professional members of the unit team but, for many of them, it also extended, as we have reported, to the acquisition and use of other resources for the buildings in the units, both material and human.

One of the unit directors perhaps accurately summarised the situation from the perspective of his peers in the following comment: 'The unit direct-ors are figureheads but have no authority. This has its effect on the building staff. There is poor morale amongst building staff which has negative consequences for the residents' care.' This is not greatly at variance with much of the evidence gathered in this research. We have indicated that in areas where the unit directors did perceive themselves to have authority, in some cases they involved their building supervisors in decisions relating to these areas. The building supervisors' perception of participation in decision making we have also shown to be positively correlated with resident-oriented care, as were more frequent meetings between them and the unit directors. It is obviously only when middle-line managers like the unit directors have some authority to delegate and some control over resources needed to plan programmes and activities that there is any possibility of their involving and influencing the activities of their presumed subordinates. If these managers get little or no support from their superiors it is not surprising in organisational terms that there is, as one assistant superintendent put it, 'chaos'. More importantly, that chaos is reflected in the diversity of the organisational characteristics of the buildings housing the residents, which we have seen are related to care practices which are themselves very variable.

Part Six
CONCLUSIONS

14 CONCLUSIONS AND RECOMMENDATIONS

We have presented a picture of the complexity and diversity of institutional life. Our data in part tell a sad and cautionary tale. These same data, however, enable us to suggest strategies that could improve the residential care of the mentally retarded, not least in institutions like those we studied but also, we think, in other residential facilities provided for them. We now try to summarise our findings and outline their implications for residential care.

Unitisation

The sad and cautionary tale to which we referred above is that of unitisation, at least as it was implemented in the settings in which we worked. It promised many things to many people. In one of the proposals we saw for the implementation of unitisation it was to generate (amongst other things) the design of individual programmes for the residents, to which rapid adjustments could be made as effective responses to the residents' needs; it would improve communication between staff, and between the institutions and surrounding community services and parents. All these were to be the consequence of the appointment of unit directors with a substantial amount of authority, and the constituting of the unit team. As we have seen, the unit directors were not in practice given a great deal of authority. They hardly could be, when the legislature, in order to effect financial savings, changed their grading from one equivalent to that of department heads to a much lower level and continued to operate a budget procedure which took no regard of the subdivision of the institutions into units or the appointment of these unit directors. We do not know whether having unit directors equal in grading to department heads would have made any difference to the organisation of the buildings which were part of their units. We only know that they were not, and that their unit teams were comprised in an uneven manner, only sometimes constituted so that the same group of specialist staff worked together to plan for the residents in a unit. In the institutions we observed unitisation produces little of demonstrable benefit, for all the energy expended by the unit directors. While this administrative innovation was not a success, we can still learn more positive lessons by considering the implications of our other findings about these organisations.

155

Strategies for Improving Care

As we noted above, our work in these institutions suggested to us strategies which appear useful in improving care in these residential facilities
for the mentally retarded, along with those that appear unproductive.
We have pointed to some of these in our discussion of the data in preceding chapters. Here we summarise those strategies arising out of our work
which we think may be of direct use to the providers of care.

1. *Recruitment and Promotional Policies and Training of Care Staff*

Altering staff recruitment or screening policies to take account of age or
sex of potential care staff does *not* seem the way to improve care. These
demographic attributes of the care staff in our study appear relatively
trivial as general determinants of care-giving. We cannot however assess
the importance of personality factors which other workers have stressed
(Butterfield & Warren, 1962, for example) for we did not attempt to
gather such information. It may be that such factors would identify
those staff who can withstand the strong pressures in these institutions
(from the residents and the organisation itself) to practise care in a
routine fashion. It is certainly clear that staff of any age or sex who continue to work in these settings appear to risk becoming as institutionalised as any resident in any custodial setting we have encountered. Their
enthusiasm wanes, they feel less involved in their work, and they accept
the values of their longer-service peers.

Promotion, even to the undizzy heights of charge attendant, has, we
have shown, some beneficial consequences for care provided, and oper-
ates as a leaven even when staff are over the magic age of 30. Obviously,
however, not everyone can be promoted. Other strategies for reducing
the institutionalisation of staff need to be developed. One such strategy
could be the assignment of staff, after a year's work in a residence, to
another location in the facility. Perhaps before such a transfer it would
be better to send a percentage of staff in each building for training or
refresher courses, giving them a chance to get out, expand their skills
and knowledge, and bring that refreshed enthusiasm back into their
original residence or some other.

Most of the care staff we studied had no training of any consequence.
What little they did possess seemed uninfluential in terms of care practices. We have no doubt that training can make some contribution to
resident-oriented care. It must however be training which is of relevance
to the work the care staff have to do, and the lessons of which they can
implement once back in the residential facility. Training could be used as a
basis for promotion *within* the residence. Alone, however, it cannot have

a positive effect on care practices. It is necessary to provide a context in which any instrumental value training might have can produce positive effects. It is essential that supportive structures are established and maintained to reduce the stress on staff who work directly with the residents, if these staff are to sustain resident-oriented care.

2. *Involvement of Care Staff in Decision Making*

One attribute of the organisational structure could contribute much to providing a supportive work situation for care staff. We have repeatedly shown that decentralisation of authority, that is the involvement in decision making of both direct-care workers and their immediate supervisors, the building heads, has positive consequences for the care of the residents. We can see no reason why these staff cannot be actively encouraged to participate in deciding such simple matters as their vacations, days off, the tasks they will do, and the development of programmes and ordering of the day's events for the residents. These are not exactly high-level policy issues, yet it was involvement in issues such as these that differentiated resident-oriented from institution-oriented buildings in our study. The implementation of such an administrative strategy can only result in positive consequences for staff and residents, and it does not seem to us to be beyond the ability of administrators to ensure that this happens.

3. *Communication between Residence Staff*

We know that increasing the frequency of communication between supervisory members of different shifts in these residences has beneficial consequences for the care the residents receive. If shift systems have to operate, either because of the demands of the legislature or of an occupational group, it is surely not inconceivable that something more than the perfunctory 'hand over' from one shift to another can occur. To organise daily inter-shift meetings necessitates some effort, but frequent meetings between these groups can have only beneficial consequences for both staff and residents.

4. *Communication between Residence Staff and Others*

We have observed that in these settings frequent meetings with the unit directors had beneficial consequences for the care the building staff provided. By frequent here we mean every day. Both the care staff and the middle-line manager or specialist stand to gain from such meetings. Meetings between these groups, so long as they are not perfunctory inspections, can provide the latter with knowledge about residents accessible only to building staff because of their daily contact with residents.

Such knowledge is invaluable in the development and modification of any individual programme. For care staff such meetings can provide an opportunity to become involved in planning programmes for the residents in their care and decisions about them. We have shown that in these settings communication on a frequent basis between these unit directors and building supervisors was related to the latter's perception of their involvement in decision making. The more they met the more they felt they were involved in decision making, and we repeat again that this sense of involvement in decision making is of great importance in the promotion of resident-oriented care.

Our evidence about frequent contact with specialist staff other than the unit director led us to question a number of assumptions that are generally made about this group. It will be recalled that as far as building heads were concerned the more frequently they met with members of eight specialist groups providing services within the institutions, the more institution-oriented the care in their building was. Further, higher levels of such contact were associated with lower feelings of staff involvement, and less perceived freedom from constraining formal rules. It is, we think, assumed that such people as doctors, nurses, psychologists, and social workers, for example, by definition espouse only what is good. Reflecting on the training of these various groups, we do not know if anything in their training (*a*) emphasises the importance of resident-oriented care; and (*b*) emphasises the importance of communicating in such a way as to be both intelligible and to present useful suggestions to people working at the direct-care level. We suggested earlier that what may well be more important than frequency of visits to residences by these groups is what they say and do when they get there. We did not study this, and it needs to be examined. What our findings do suggest is that simply pumping in more and more specialists (who cost quite a lot) probably will not improve care at residence level, on the dimensions we measured, one jot.

5. *Working Relationships between Building Supervisors and Direct-Care Staff*

Within the residences themselves, relationships between the two levels of staff have consequences for the care provided in particular ways. First, for the direct-care staff, the less they feel constrained by written rules and regulations the more they perceive themselves as involved in decision making, in the limited number of matters we have mentioned above. We are convinced, from the weight of our evidence, that these feelings of participation are crucial to care, and thus mechanisms to promote them are very important.

We know too that the residence supervisors' activities influence the care-taking practices of the direct-care workers. When a building head actively engages in more activity directly involving the residents, this is associated with lower specialisation between the two levels of building staff. The lower the level of specialisation of task within the buildings, the more resident-oriented is the speech used by direct-care staff to the residents.

6. *The Clients*

We described how we conceptualised the characteristics of the residents as attributes defining the work situation of the building staff. We noted that the age and sex of the residents contributed nothing to the variance we found in the care provided for them. However, we have repeatedly emphasised the negative consequences of exclusively grouping profoundly and severely retarded residents together. Such a practice (alas part of what was called unitisation in these settings, but surely not a necessary ingredient of it, since there are other criteria for grouping people together) appeared to guarantee institution-oriented care for these clients, no matter which of our dimensions we examined. We can only reiterate the disastrous consequences of this policy. We do not know what kind of mixed grouping, that is what ratio of profoundly and severely retarded residents to mildly and moderately retarded residents, will, if any will, improve the level of care for the handicapped. We do know for sure that the less able, if they are grouped together, seem to get less in every way.

We also showed the significance of the number of residents to be cared for in so far as everyday management practices were concerned. Our evidence indicates that any grouping of more than 30 residents, no matter what their level of ability, can only have deleterious consequences for their care. We have no evidence that staffing ratios are an important factor in the kind of care the residents receive. Clearly by this we do not mean that 29 residents can be cared for by one member of staff and all will be well. Such an argument is sheer nonsense. What seems to us important in discussing staffing ratios is a consideration of the dependence level and needs of the residents, and only when these have been determined can any sensible accounting of this issue be made.

7. *The Multi-dimensionality of Care and Care-taking*

One major implication of our work is the clear demonstration that care and care-taking in these residential facilities is *not* unidimensional. We were able to show that three different dimensions of care are at least moderately distinct: daily management of routine and recurring events, staff speech to the residents, and the quality of the physical environment. Whilst we were not able to show that contact with the community was statistically independent of the measure we used to quantify the first dimension, we think it is worth consideration in its own right. Any meaningful strategy to improve care, by which we mean make it more resident-oriented, will have to involve proposals on each of these fronts. It is futile to talk about improving care as if it were all of one piece. Where care may be resident-oriented on one dimension of those we have measured, it is not necessarily so on another.

Before care can be effectively improved in these settings or any other residential facility for the mentally handicapped, policy makers need a clearly established plan which takes account of the diversity of the needs of the mentally handicapped. A plan, that is, which does not merely reflect a current ideology espoused by a particularly vociferous pressure group, whether academic or parental. These policy makers too must be aware that political decisions about numbers of staff, or the grades and types of staff allocated, will have a great impact on what is feasible in the provision of care. They should also be aware of the complexity of the interrelationships within the structure of these facilities so that no single administrative strategy can be proposed as a panacea for all ills; for in our detailed findings we have shown how different aspects of the organisation's structure and the attributes of the people who work in the buildings are significant for one dimension of care, but not for another. A simple example is the fact that frequent communication between shifts at building supervisor level is not associated with the speech used to residents but does have a positive effect on the management of daily and recurring events. The more frequent the meetings, the more resident-oriented the care on this dimension. Thus to make improvements by making changes in the organisational structure of residential facilities, it is again too simplistic to assume that by changing one aspect of that structure, for example the extent to which staff are involved in meetings, global improvements in every aspect of care will be effected. Attention will have to be paid to several features of the organisation's structure—participation in decision making, formalisation, the role of the middle-line manager, promotion systems and communication, for example. All of them, as we have indicated, have implications for the care staff *and* the care they provide. Without a supportive organisational structure for care staff innovations to improve the quality of care will neither endure nor contribute much to raise the standard of care.

We hope that what we have written will have dispelled some of the sociological and other myths about institutions and pointed to more rational ways of characterising residential institutions. We also hope it will assist policy makers and those who provide residential services to make informed decisions in their attempts to improve these services.

APPENDIX 1. QUESTIONNAIRES AND OBSERVATION SCHEDULES

RESIDENT CHARACTERISTICS

Name _____   Building _____

If X is not in building as listed,   Case _____
where is he/she?_____

---

1. Sex

   Male..............................
   Female............................

2. Date of Birth _____

3. Age

   0   -   5..........................
   6   - 11..........................
   12 - 15..........................
   16 - 18..........................
   19 - 25..........................
   26 - 36..........................
   37 - 50..........................
   51 - 60..........................
   61 - 70..........................
   71 + ...

4. I.Q.

   Normal   85-...................
   Borderline 70-84.................
   Mild   55-69.................
   Moderate   40-54.................
   Severe   25-39.................
   Profound   0-24..................
   No Information.....................

5. Date of Admission

   Less than 6 months.................
   6 months, less than 1 year.........
   1 year, less than 2 years..... ......
   2 years, less than 3 years.........
   3 years, less than 4 years.........
   4 years, less than 5 years.........
   5 years, less than 10 years........
   10 years or more...................

6a. Does X go to any organized activities
    outside the building during the day?

    Community Work Placement-FT.........
    Community Work Placement-PT.........
    On Grds.   Work Placement-FT.........
    On Grds.   Work Placement-PT.........
    Workshop (On Grds.)-FT..............
    Workshop (On Grds.)-PT..............
    Voc. Training (Off Grds.)-FT........
    Voc. Training (Off Grds.)-PT........

6a.(Cont.):

    School (On Grds.)-FT................
    School (On Grds.)-PT................
    School (Off Grds.)-FT..............
    School (Off Grds.)-PT..............
    Building-FT........................
    Other Programs (Off Grds.)-FT......
    Other Programs (Off Grds.)-PT......
    Other Programs (On Grds.)-FT.......
    Other Programs (On Grds.)-PT.......
    Other..............................

6b.When X is in the building is he
   involved in self-help programs?
   How often?

   Daily..............................
   Weekly.............................
   Rarely or never....................

6c.When X is in the building is he
   involved in academic programs?
   How often?

   Daily..............................
   Weekly.............................
   Rarely or never....................

6d.When X is in the building is he
   involved in recreational activities?
   How often?

   Daily..............................
   Weekly.............................
   Rarely or never....................

6e.When X is in the building does he
   have a job?   How often?

   Daily..............................
   Weekly.............................
   Rarely or never....................

6f.(No activity or job in the building.)

   Yes...................... ....
   No.................................

7. Can X walk unaided?

Walks unaided (includes stairs)....
Walks with help: e.g. ....
  Staff_____ Cane _____
  Walker _____ Prosthesis_____
Uses wheelchair and able to move
  in it unaided (more than 50% of
  the day).........................
Shuffles on bottom, crawls, etc....
Bedfast - has to be carried........
Other..............................

8. Can X feed himself?

Feeds self with knife and fork
  without supervision..............
Feeds self with knife and fork
  with supervision.................
Feeds self with spoon or fork
  without supervision..............
Feeds self with spoon or fork
  with supervision.................
Feeds self with fingers only.......
Has to be fed at table or
  wheelchair.......................
Has to be fed in bed...... ....
Other.............................. .....

9. Can X dress and undress himself?

Dresses and undresses self unaided.
Dresses self with supervision......
Dresses and undresses self except
  for buttons, snaps, zippers,
  shoelaces........................
Needs some help....................
Has to be dressed completely.......
Other..............................

10. Can X brush and comb his own hair?

Does own unaided...................
Needs supervision..................
Needs some help....................
Has to be done for resident........
Has no hair........................
Other..............................

11. Can X clean his own teeth?

Cleans own unaided (Dentures___)...
Needs supervision..................
Needs some help....................
Has to be done for resident........
No teeth...........................
No toothbrush......................
Other..............................

12. Does X wet himself during the day?

Rarely or never wets..............
Wets at least once a month........
Wets at least once a week.........
Wets daily........................
Catheterized......................
Other (specify)...................

13. Does X soil during the day?

Soils rarely or never.............
Soils at least once a month.......
Soils at least once a week........
Soils at least once a day.........
Colostomy.........................
Other (specify)...................

14. Does X wet or soil himself during
the night?

Is wet and/or soils rarely or
  never...........................
Is wet and/or soils at least once
  a month.........................
Is wet and/or soils at least once
  a week..........................
Is wet and/or soils at least once
  a night.........................
Catheterized......................
Colostomy.........................
Other.............................

15. Can X use the toilet by himself
(undressing, sitting, paper,
flushing, dressing)?

Toilets self unaided including
  toilet paper....................
Toilets self unaided; toilet
  paper not available.............
Needs supervision.................
Has to be done for resident.......
Uses bedpan unaided...............
Uses bedpan with total help.......
Catheterised......................
Doubly incontinent................
Other.............................

16. Can X wash and shower himself
(soaps, rinses, towels)?

Washes and showers self unaided...
Washes and showers self with
  supervision.....................
Washes but cannot shower self
  unaided.........................
Washes and showers self with some
  help............................
Has to be washed and showered.....
Other.............................

17. Can X shampoo his own hair (soap
    or shampoo on head, lathers,
    rinses off)?

    Shampoos own hair.................
    Needs supervision.................
    Needs some help...................
    Has to be done for resident.......
    No hair...........................
    Other.............................

18. Is X's hearing normal?

    Normal hearing (with aid)____......
    Poor hearing............. ....
    Deaf or almost....................
    Other.............................

19. Is X's sight normal?

    Normal sight (with glasses)____....
    Poor sight........................
    Blind or almost...................
    Other.............................

20. Can X read?

    Reads simple printed material or
      more............................
    Reads single words and/or some
      signs...........................
    Recognises own name...............
    Reads single letters only.........
    Can't read single letters.........
    Other.............................

21. Can X write?

    Can write at least simple letters
      to family or friends............
    Can write simple words only.......
    Can write own name only...........
    Can write single letters only.....
    Can copy letters, words or name
      only............................
    Cannot form words or letters......
    Other.............................

22. Can X tell the time by the clock?

    Accurately........................
    Within the hour...................
    Not at all........................
    Other.............................

23. Does X know his money?

    Can count change to ∮.............
    Knows some equivalences of coins..
    Names at least some coins.........
    No indication of money skills.....
    No information....................
    Other..... ....

24. Can X talk?

    Uses complete grammatical sentences
      mainly..........................
    Uses phrases mainly...............
    Uses some phrases and single words....
    Uses single words only............
    Uses no recognisable words........
    Mute..............................
    Other.............................

25a. Can you understand X when he speaks?

    Yes, all of what he says..........
    Most of what he says; 50% or more....
    Some of what he says; less than 50%..
    No words..........................
    Other.............................

25b. Could I understand him when he speaks?

    Yes, all of what he says..........
    Most of what he says; 50% or more....
    Some of what he says; less than 50%..
    No words..........................
    Other.............................

26. Does X understand when you tell him
    to get something and take it
    someplace?

    Understands whole commands.........
    Understands one part of command only..
    Understands one-or two-word action
      commands only...................
    Recognises own name only..........
    Doesn't recognise own name........
    Other.............................

27. Does X hit out or attack others?

    Does not apply....... ....
    Somewhat applies; less than weekly
      more than once or twice.........
    Applies; less than daily, at least
      once a week.....................
    Certainly applies; daily or more.....

28. Is X extremely overactive?

    Does not apply....................
    Somewhat applies; less than weekly
      more than once or twice.........
    Applies; less than daily, at least
      once a week.....................
    Certainly applies; daily or more.....

29. Is X constantly seeking attention
    will not leave staff alone?

    Does not apply......... ....
    Somewhat applies; less than weekly
      more than once or twice.. ......
    Applies; less than daily, at least
      once a week.....................
    Certainly applies, daily or more......

30. Does X tear up paper, clothing, or damage furniture, windows, toys?

Does not apply......................
Somewhat applies; less than weekly more than once or twice............
Applies; less than daily, at least once a week.......................
Certainly applies, daily or more....

31. Is X constantly injuring self, e.g., head banging, picking sores?

Does not apply......................
Somewhat applies; less than weekly more than once or twice............
Applies less than daily, at least once a week... ....
Certainly applies, daily or more....

32. Does X have temper tantrums and/or screaming fits?

Does not apply... ....
Somewhat applies, less than weekly more than once or twice............
Applies; less than daily, at least once a week.....................
Certainly applies, weekly or more...

33. Does X leave the school grounds without permission?

Does not apply ....
Somewhat applies, less than monthly more than once or twice...........
Applies; less than weekly, at least once a month....................
Certainly applies; weekly or more..

34. Does X steal things?

Does not apply.....................
Somewhat applies; less than monthly more than once or twice...........
Applies; less than weekly, at least once a month....................
Certainly applies, weekly or more...

35. Does X refuse to keep his clothes on?

Does not apply.....................
Somewhat applies; less than monthly, more than once or twice...........
Applies; less than weekly, at least once a month.....................
Certainly applies; weekly or more...

36. Could I check whether X possesses the following items? (Check if YES)

____Underwear

____Shirt or blouse

____Pants or skirt

____Dress, suit, or jacket

____Sweater

____Overcoat

____Pair of shoes

____Pyjamas

____Bathrobe

____Slippers

____Total number of above items

RESIDENTS' DAY

I want to talk to you about day to day and other aspects of the residents care.
It would help me to understand better the work you have to do and how you do it.
If for some reason you don't know what happens please just say so.   As in my other
conversations with you everything you say will be confidential.

1. Can I just check the number of residents currently here.   N =

2. How many employees were on duty   N

    (a) yesterday from 7   - 3.30 ....

    (b)   "   " 2.30-11   ....

    (c)   "   " 11   - 7   ....

    (d) yesterday for other periods _____

    (e) don't know ....

3. What time did the residents start getting up yesterday

    (Record time or period) from _____ to _____

    Don't know ....

4. Were they all out of bed when you got here?

    Yes ....

    No ....

    Don't know ....

*5. Do they all get up at this time at weekends
        too?
    Yes all...

    Yes some.. ....

    No all different..

    Don't know.............

6. What time did you serve breakfast yesterday.   Is it always at this time.
    When did it finish.   Is this the same each day.

    Begins .... Same time   Varies
    Finishes .... Same time   Varies
    Don't know ....

7. Where is this eaten.   Is this the same for all meals

    Dining room ....   All meals ....   Some meals

    Dormitory ....   All meals ....   Some meals

    Other _____   All meals ....   Some meals

    Don't know ....

8. When were the residents showered or supervised in showering yesterday.
    Is it at the same time each day.

    Before breakfast   Every day...........   Varies.......

    After breakfast   Every day...........   Varies.......

    Before supper   Every day...........   Varies.......

    After supper   Every day...........   Varies.......

    DNA no-one showered ....

    Don't know ....

9. When do the residents who shower themselves do this?   Is this always the
    same time

    Before breakfast   Every day...........   Varies.......

    After breakfast   Every day...........   Varies.......

    Before supper   Every day...........   Varies.......

    After supper   Every day...........   Varies.......

    DNA no one showers self...............................

    Don't know..

10. Where do they get soap and towels from

                                                        Soap   Towel

    Keep their own..

    Ask attendants..

    Available in cupboards etc. ....

    Available in bathroom............. ... .

    Don't know..

11. Were any of the residents toileted or supervised in this yesterday morning.
    Was this before or after breakfast.   Is it the same tim each day.

    Before breakfast   Every day.............   Varies.....

    After breakfast   Every day.............   Varies.....

    DNA no-one supervised or helped.......................

    Don't know...

12. Are there any residents who use the toilet without supervision.   How do
    they get toilet paper.

    DNA no-one uses toilet unsupervised...................................

    There is none...

    Ask staff...

    Available in cupboard...

    Available in stalls...

    Don't know........................

13. Did anyone leave the building yesterday to go to school or work etc.   What
    time did they go and how many went.   When did they come back.

    Time leave ------------------- N   Time return -------------- N

    Time   "   ------------------- N   Time   "   -------------- N

    Time   "   ------------------- N   Time   "   -------------- N

    DNA no-one goes ....

    Don't know ....

14. Were the ones who were left here doing anything yesterday morning after
    breakfast until lunch time.

    Showering & toileting .... All   Some   None

    Watching TV .... All   Some   None

    Table activities .... All   Some   None

    Sitting about .... All   Some   None

    Seeing professionals .... All   Some   None

    Seeing parents .... All   Some   None

    Going for walks .... All   Some   None

    Games/reading/listen to radio .... All   Some   None

    Sleeping .... All   Some   None

14.(Cont.):

Other ------------------------------- All   Some   None

DNA no-one left....................

Don't know ....

15.What time did the midday meal arrive yesterday

Time -------------------------------

Don't know ....

16.What time did you serve lunch yesterday. How many residents were here.
When did it finish.

Time begun -------------------------

Number ....

Time finished ----------------------

17.Did anyone leave the building yesterday after lunch for work or school.
What time was this at. What time do they come back.

Time leave	---------------------- N	Time return	-------------- N
Time "	---------------------- N	Time "	-------------- N
Time "	---------------------- N	Time "	-------------- N
Time "	---------------------- N	Time "	-------------- N
Time "	---------------------- N	Time "	-------------- N

DNA no-one goes ....

Don't know ....

18.After lunch yesterday, what were the residents doing until you left

Showering & toileting .... All   Some   None

Watching TV .... All   Some   None

Table activities .... All   Some   None

Sitting about .... All   Some   None

Seeing professionals .... All   Some   None

Seeing parents .... All   Some   None

Going for walks .... All   Some   None

Games/reading/listen to radio .... All   Some   None

18. (Cont.):

Sleeping .... All   Some   None

Other ------------------------------ All   Some   None

DNA no-one left ....

Don't know ....

19. Do you know what time supper was served yesterday?

Yes, time ---------------------------

Don't know ....

20. Do you know what time the residents went to bed yesterday

Time: from ----------- to -----------

Don't know ....

21. Do they all go to bed at this time at weekends too?

Yes all ....

Yes some ....

No all different ....

Don't know ....

22. Do you know how many residents are toileted at night and how many times.

All once or more ....

Some more than once ....

None or some once only ....

Don't know ....

*
23. Did you or any of the other attendants sit down and watch TV with the residents yesterday.   Does this happen every day?

Everyday ....

Less often but at least once a week ....

Less often than once a week ....

DNA, no television ....

24. Do you find it necessary to keep any rooms or storage areas locked for at least part of the day.

Which are these

None locked..

24. (Cont.):

   Yes, list areas —————————————————

   ——————————————————————

   ——————————————————————

*25. How many residents do you allow into the kitchen when you or other attendants are there?

   67 – 100% ....

   34 – 66% ....

   0 – 33% ....

*26. What are your rules about the times of day at which residents can use their dormitories (if no separate day room ask about beds)

   All use them whenever they like.....................................

   Used under various conditions ....

   All at set times ....

*27. What are your rules about the residents using your yard or front area during the day.

   All use it when they like ....

   Under various conditions ....

   All at set times or not at all ....

28. What are your rules about the residents coming into the office when you or other attendants are here.

   No restrictions for all residents ....

   Some residents allowed in or some restrictions ....

   All not allowed (except for special events) ....

   Kept locked ....

*29. What are your rules about visitors coming here.

   Come any time ....

   Come any day but visiting hours only ....

   Come certain days only ....

30. What do you do with clothes residents bring with them.

   All keep and use them ....

   All residents, used only on special occasions or some residents regularly used ....

   Not used or allowed for all residents ....

31. What do you do with other personal possessions the residents bring with them.

They all keep and use them ....

Some keep and use them ....

We keep them and let them use it, we keep them.   They don't bring
them ....

33. How many residents currently have personal possessions **other** than clothes
of their own, e.g. books, radio, games.

67 - 100% ....

34 - 66% ....

 0 - 33% ....

34. Do you or other attendants take residents on walks, either on grounds or off.
How often is this.

Every day ....

Weekly ....

Less often than weekly ....

Don't know ....   Residents go alone ....

35. When these walks occur does everyone go together and stay together or do they
split up or do residents go out at different times.

All go out a few at a time ....

All go out together but split into group ....

All stay together in line or don't go on walks ....

DNA ....

36. How often do your residents go to the following activities in the grounds.

	Weekly	More than once a month	Monthly or less
	N	N	N
Cinema			
Swimming			
Gym			
Dances			
Church			

37. How many of the residents have been on trips with attendants in the last 3 months.

    67 - 100% ....

    34 - 66% ....

     0 - 33% ....

38. What if anything do you do about residents birthdays.

    Everyone has an individual celebration ....

    Some have individual celebration, all others share or all share ....

    Some or all have no celebration ....

Thank you for your help.   I would like to come and see what goes on first thing
in the morning and at supper, showering and toilet times.   Would it be OK if I
just dropped in at the times you have mentioned these occur or shall I arrange
it with you now.

  Building

                                                        Ward
                                                        _____

1. __Getting up__   Day 1   Day 2   __Comments__

    (i)   Time 1st resident up

    (ii)   Time breakfast served

    (iii) Total N of residents

                           N   N   N
    (iv)   __Time__   W+D   ACT   UNO
                     Day 1 Day 2 Day 1 Day 2 Day 1 Day 2

           _____

           _____

           _____

           _____

           _____

           _____

           _____

           _____

_____

2. __Enter dining room__   Day 1   Day 2

    (i) N of residents entering
         individually

    (ii) N of residents in line or
         group outside dining room

    (iii)No separate dining room

_____

__Toileting__ (Observe when 2+ people on duty)

3. __Process__   Day 1   Day 2

    N of residents helped by 1 person

    N of residents helped by 2 or more
     people

    N of residents not helped

_____

4. <u>After toilet</u>   Day 1   Day 2

    N of residents leaving
    individually

    N of residents waiting in
    bathroom

<u>Showering</u> (Observe when 2 + people on duty)

5. <u>Activity before showering</u>   Day 1   Day 2

    N of residents occupied in
    activity

    N of residents unoccupied in
    day room or dormitory

    N of residents unoccupied in
    bathroom

6. <u>Process</u>   Day 1   Day 2

    N of residents helped with
    showering by 1 person

    N of residents helped by 2
    or more people

    N of residents not helped

---

7. <u>After bathing</u>   Day 1   Day 2

    N of residents leaving
    individually

    N of residents waiting in
    bathroom

<u>Meal Time</u>
                                                    Time
8. <u>Waiting before and after</u>   Day 1   Day 2

    1st resident sits

    1st resident eats

    1st resident finishes

    1st resident leaves table

Comments

9. Table set   Day 1   Day 2

    (i)   N of places set on trays
          with knife & fork or spoon
          & fork

    (ii) N of residents handed food
          & silverware by staff

    (iii) N of residents eating

---

10. Staff activity   Day 1   Day 2

    All staff eating with residents

    Some staff eating or sitting at
     table with residents

    All staff stand, supervise

LANGUAGE OBSERVATION SCHEDULE	Building Date: _____	Activity: CS: CF: I	Terminal command	Initial command	Information exchange	Talk other	No talk (to resident)	Target S.I.G.O.	Target reply	Staff M.C.L.	No. of Residents 1–5; 5+; 10+
Time:_____ Location:	Comment verbatim:										
1	2	3	4	5	6	7	8	9	10	11	12

DA: DR: W: B: O:
CR: H
(1).. .. . .

....

....

....

DA: DR: W: B: O:
CR: H
(2).. .. . .

....

....

....

DA: DR: W: B: O:
CR: H
(3).. .. . .

....

....

....

Staff 1 ---------------- Staff 2 --------------- Staff 3 ------------

Building code

N Residents

Date:

_____

PHYSICAL ENVIRONMENT INVENTORY

	Rough	Building N

A. <u>Rooms</u>

1. Dormitories .... _____
2. Total beds .... _____
3. Bathrooms .... _____
4. Dayrooms .... _____
5. Solariums .... _____
6. Dining rooms .... _____
7. Dining areas (between partitions) .... _____
8. Clothing rooms .... _____
9. Laundry .... _____
10. Kitchen .... _____
11. Office .... _____
12. Other (specify) _____

_____

13. Levels of building .... _____
14. Yards (enclosed) .... _____
15. Open areas adjacent to building .... _____

	Rough	Building N

B. Furnishings

16. Tables - occasional ....

17. Arm chairs ....

18. Couch/settee ....

19. Bookshelves ....

20. Games and toy cupboards ....

21. TV ....

22. Radio ....

23. Curtains/blinds (N rooms with) ....

24. Waste Bins in dayrooms, dorms, bathrooms ....

25. Washing machines ....

26. Dryers ....

27. Metal or other cabinets to store dishes in kitchen
                        (check if applicable)

28. Fridges ....

29. Stoves ....

30. Hotplates ....

31. Dishwasher ... .

32. Drinking fountains ....

C. Bathrooms

33. Toilets with: no partitions or doors ....

34.   with partitions only ....

35.   with partitions and doors ....

36.   total toilets ....

37. Showers: no partitions or doors/curtains ....

38.   with partition only ....

39.   with partitions and doors/curtains ....

40.   total showers .. ..

	Rough	Building N

C. Bathrooms (Cont:)

41. Bath tubs: no doors or partitions ....

42.   partitions only ....

43.   partitions and doors/curtains,
                        or separate room ....

44.   total tubs ....

45. Slabs ....

46. Handbasins ....

47. Mirrors ....

48. Toilet paper (N bathrooms with) ....

D. Dormitories

49. N beds per dorm ....

50. Beds with drawers..........................

51. Bedside lockers ....

52. Floor coverings (carpets/mats) ....

53. Mirrors ....

54. Curtains or blinds (N dorms with) ....

55. Bedspreads: N dorms with ....

56.   N dorms with different spreads
                  in them ....

57. Pictures: (N dorms with)

	Dorms	Building

                  pinups, personal photos or
                  paintings ....

                  posters & other non-resident art
                  pinned on walls ....

                  murals ....

60. RMP score from 52a

                  In all rooms ....

                  In some rooms ....

                  In no rooms ....

	Dorms	Building

E. Daily Clothing Storage (N = basic storage units)

61. Individual chest of drawers and/or closet .... _____

62. Shared cupboard or chest .... _____

63. Labelled locker or box in clothing room .... _____

64. All together in clothing room or laundry box OR
    put on bed (check) .... _____

65. CMS score from E

           In private provision .... _____

           In shared provision .... _____

           In communal provision .... _____

   Yard

66. Benches .... _____

67. Fixed playthings .... _____

68. Plants & trees (check if applicable) .... _____

69. Grassed   (check if applicable) .... _____

70. Railing/fence (check if applicable) .... _____

Building

N Residents

Date: -------------------

RESIDENTS COMMUNITY CONTACTS

I would like to find out the extent to which residents are involved in activities outside.   The information you give me will be treated as confidential.

	Total	Don't know
1. How many residents went to boy/girl scouts in the last month?		
2. How many residents went shopping (for clothes) in the last month?		
3. How many residents went to the movies in the last month?		
4. How many residents went to a museum in the last month?		
5. How many residents have been on a public bus in the last month?		
6. How many went to a restaurant or cafeteria in the last month?		
7. How many went to a house other than that of their parents for a visit in the last month?		
8. How many have been for a car ride in the last month?		
9. How many have been to religious services off the grounds in the last month?		
10. Could you tell me from your record book how many residents have been on overnight visits home or elsewhere in the last month?		

	Total	Don't know

11. How many residents went to the hairdresser or
    barber off the grounds in the last 6 months?...

12. How many went to visit a doctor or dentist off
    the grounds in the last 6 months? ....

13. How many residents went on an (annual) holiday
    in the last year?

    (a) with the family? ....

    (b) organised by the school or other?..........

DIRECT CARE STAFF   Code number

_____

This questionnaire is strictly confidential.   It will not be shown to anyone
outside the research team.   There are no right or wrong answers, only those
which apply to you.   Please answer by placing check marks in the appropriate
boxes.

_____

Please check <u>one or more</u> boxes for each part of this question:

1. In your building who is usually involved in deciding:	Attend-ants	Charges	Building Matron or equiv-alent	Unit Dir-ector	Profession-al staff (teachers, social workers, doctors, etc.
(a) what tasks attendants do for the residents					
(b) what housekeeping and cleaning jobs attendants do					
(c) when attendant can take their vacation, days off, etc.					

Please check <u>one</u> box for each
part of this question

2. How often do you talk about residents problems or programmes with any of the following?	Most days	About once a week	About once a month	Less often or never
(a) attendants on other shifts in your building				
(b) the building Matron or equivalent				
(c) the Unit Director				
(d) Professional Staff (teachers, social workers, doctors, etc.)				

3. Do you go to building meetings: Yes, about once a week

                                       Yes, about once a month

                                       Yes, but only occasionally

                                       No, never

Please check one box for each part of this question

4. How much do you find that each of the following groups help you in your work?	Very helpful	Helpful	Average	Un-helpful	Very Unhelp-ful
(a) Other shifts in your building					
(b) Professional staff (teachers, social workers, doctors,etc.)					
(c) Service employees (kitchen, garage, maintenance, etc.)					

5. Do you have a written job description?

Yes

No

6. Have you been given any written rules about your work?

Yes

No

7. Have you had any in-service training in the last year?

Yes

No

8a. When did you start work in this building?

_____
Month   Year

8b. When did you start work at Fernald?

_____
Month   Year

9. Who is your immediate superior?   Don't know

Charge

Matron

Head Nurse

Unit Director

Other

_____

Please would you answer the following questions about yourself:

10. Age: Under 20   21-30   31-40   41-50   51 and over

11. Sex: Male   Female

12. Marital Status: Single   Married   Divorced

13. Do you live on the school grounds?   Yes

                                             No

14. Do you have any formal qualifications related to working with the retarded?

                     No

                     Yes   What is this?

                     _____

                     _____

15. In every kind of organisation people run into problems.   Would you write
    down what you find to be the main problems in doing your job?

16. Are there any things which you would like to see changed here?

THANK YOU VERY MUCH FOR YOUR HELP

1974

<u>BUILDING HEADS</u>

Building

Staff

_____

I want to talk to you about the organisation of your building and your role in this. All of your replies will be treated as strictly confidential and not shown to anyone outside the Research Team.

1. I have a list of people working in your building, could we go through it and

    (a) check that the hours and days off are correct
    (b) if there are any additions, and hours and days off of these people
    (c) if anyone is no longer here
    (d) if all the night staff are included

Name	(1) Position	(2) Hours	(3)	(4) Days off

2. Could you tell me if any of the following staff are assigned to your building and also how often they visit you.

	MD	Psycho- logist	SW	Teacher	OT	PT	Rehab.	RN	LPN
Assigned									
Not Assigned									
Daily Visit									
Weekly Visit									
Less Often than Weekly									
Rarely or Never									

3. How often does the Unit Director visit your building to speak with you

  At least once a day

  At least once a week

  Less often than weekly

  Rarely or never

  No Unit Director

4. Do any other members of the administration visit you

	Superintendent	Asst. Sup.	Asst. Sup.	Asst Sup.	Other
Daily					
Weekly					
Less often than weekly					
Rarely or never					

5. Are there any meetings between the morning and afternoon shift.   How often
    do these take place.

    Daily ....

    Weekly ....

    Monthly ....

    Less often than monthly, never .....

    (If never check not applicable in Q.7 and Q.8 and go to Q.9)

6. Do all the staff go to these meetings

    Only senior people (charges, supervisors, matrons) ....
    Only senior people and a few others ....
    Yes most ....
    Yes all ....
    Not applicable ....

7. What is discussed at these meetings

    Problems about a specific resident ....
    General problems relating to residents ....
    Domestic problems e.g. cleaning, laundry ....
    Administrative or staff problems ....
    Other ....
    Not applicable ....

8. Do you go to any (other) regular meetings.   How often and who else comes.
    What do you discuss.

(1) Frequency and Name	(2) Content			(3) Others attending
	Residents	Staff & Admin- istration	Domestic & Maintenance	

9. Who has the authority to hire attendants for your building

   I do ....
   I am always consulted ....
   I am sometimes consulted ....
   I am rarely or never consulted...

10. Who has the authority to fire attendants in your building

    I do ....
    I am always consulted ....
    I am sometimes consulted ....
    I am rarely or never consulted...

11. Who has the authority to determine what jobs your attendants will do

    I do ....
    I am always consulted ....
    I am sometimes consulted ....
    I am rarely or never consulted...

12. Are you involved in ordering any of the following equipment for your building

Item	(1) I do this alone	(2) I do this in consultation with UD	(3) My Supervisor does it	(4) I never do it a subordinate does it
Linens				
Crockery				
New clothes for residents				
New furniture				
New TV, refrigerator				
Food other than meals				
Getting repairs done				

13. Who has authority to admit residents to your building

    I do ....
    I am always consulted ....
    I am sometimes consulted........
    I am rarely or never consulted...

14a. Who has the authority to decide when a resident is transferred from your building?

14b. Who has the authority to decide when a resident is discharged from your building?

    I do ....
    I am always consulted ....
    I am sometimes consulted ....
    I am rarely or never consulted...

15. Who has the authority to decide any of the following

	I never do it a subordinate does it	I do this alone	I do this in consultation with UD always	I do this in consultation with UD sometimes	My Supervisor does it	Other
(a) When attendants have days off						
(b) When attendants have vacation						
(c) When residents get up						
(d) When residents go to bed						
(e) Meal times						
(f) When residents can go home on leave						

16a. Are any records on the residents kept in the building

    No, all records kept elsewhere
    Yes, some records kept in building
    Yes, all records kept in building

16b. What are these   16c. Who has access to them

_____

_____

_____

_____

_____

_____

_____

_____

_____

_____

17. Are there any programs being run in the building by professional staff

    Yes

    No

18. Are you consulted by the professional staff about setting up programs in
   the building

    Yes, I am always consulted ....

    Yes, I am sometimes consulted......

    No, rarely ....

    DNA there aren't any ....

19. Are any building staff involved in running these programs

    Yes, at least one building staff member is always involved ......

    Sometimes building staff are involved ....

    Building staff have nothing to do with it ....

20. Are you consulted about the placement of residents on new programmes outside
   the building? (e.g. school, training, work)

    Yes, I am always consulted ....

    Yes, I am sometimes consulted ....

    No, rarely ....

    DNA there aren't any ....

21. There are a number of School Services like the Kitchen, the Laundry, etc.
    As I go down a list of these could you tell me whether you rate their
    services to your building as good, average, or poor.   If you don't use
    the services please say so.

Service	(1) Good	(2) Average	(3) Poor	(4) DNA
Bakery				
Kitchen				
Storeroom				
Garage				
Housekeeping				
Laundry				
Grounds				
Repair & maintenance				
Security				
Engineering				

22. Please check one box for each part of this question.

22a. How much do you find that each of the following groups help you in your work?	Very helpful	Helpful	Average	Un- helpful	Very un- helpful
(a) Other shifts in your building					
(b) Professional staff (teachers, social workers, doctors,etc.)					
(c)Service employees (kitchen, garage, maintenance, etc.)					
(d)The administration					

22b. Do you think that there are adequate programmes
     for the residents?

                                                    Yes

                                                    No

23. In every kind of organisation people run into problems.   Could you say what
    you find to be the main problems in your job.

24. Are there any things you would like to see changed here.

25. Can you tell me what your goals are for your building.

26. Has unitisation added any activities to your job.

27. Has unitisation removed any activities from your job.   Who does these now.

28. Do you think unitisation increased or decreased your authority

    Increased

    Decreased

    Stayed same

Now would you mind telling me

29. How old you are

30. When you started work in your
    present position

30a. When did you start work in
     this building

31. What was your last educational
    qualification

    College graduate

    High School graduate

    High School

    Other (specify) ....

32. Have you had any in-service
    training in the last year

        Yes
        No

33. Record sex

        Male
        Female

34. Marital status

        Married
        Single
        Widowed Divorced

35. Place of residence

        Off grounds
        On grounds

36. Is there anything else you would like
    to add to what we've discussed about
    the problems of running a building?

                THANK YOU VERY MUCH FOR YOUR HELP

ROLE SPECIALISATION

Building

Date ------------------

Time began: ---------------------

Sheet number: --------

1 S	2 Activity	3 Code	4 S-R interaction	5 C	6 R	7 Tol	8 A	9 T	10 P	11 RP

1

2

3

Unit _____

UNIT ORGANISATION SCHEDULE

I want to talk to you about the organisation of your Unit, the way it is
administered, the practical problems you have.   Before we begin, I'd like to
assure you that all your replies will be treated as strictly confidential.

1. Can I begin by checking the names of the buildings that make up your Unit.

_____

_____

_____

_____

_____

_____

2. Can you tell me who is in overall charge of these on (a) day shift, (b)
    afternoon shift, and (c) night shift.

Buildings	AM	PM	Night

_____

_____

_____

_____

_____

_____

3. Do you hire any of the direct care staff?

4. Can you describe the hiring procedure for direct care staff.   (Probe who
    involved, who has final say.)

5. Do you hire any professional staff for your buildings.

6. If yes to Question 5, can you describe the procedure. (Probe who involved, final say.)

7. If no for some to Question 5, can you tell me how professional staff became assigned to your buildings.

Physicians

Social Workers

Psychologists

O.T.'s

Nurses

P.T.'s

Rehab.

Teachers

Others

---

8. How many people would you say are directly answerable to you in your Unit?

Building	Direct Care	Maintenance	Professional

9. Have you fired any staff who work in your Unit?

			Buildings
Direct Care	Yes	No	
Maintenance	Yes	No	
Physicians	Yes	No	
Social Workers	Yes	No	
Psychologists	Yes	No	
O.T.'s	Yes	No	
P.T.'s	Yes	No	
Rehab.	Yes	No	
Teachers	Yes	No	
Others	Yes	No	
Nurses			

10. If yes to Question 9, can you describe the procedure involved in doing this. (Probe who else involved, who has final say.)

11. Do you have a budget for your Unit?   Yes

                                            No

12. If yes to Question 11, can you tell me for what things you have this and how it is drawn up.   (Probe who involved, final say)

13. Can you tell me how the following things are acquired for each of the
buildings in your Unit.   (Probe who submits order, to whom, financed,
source of material.)

Order from Central Supplies by UD 0
Order from Central Supplies by UD after consulting building staff...... 1
Order from Central Supplies by building staff subject to UD's approval. 2
Order from Central Supplies directly by building staff 3
Other 4

Building

(a) New Sheets & Towels	0 1 2 3 4	0 1 2 3 4	0 1 2 3 4	0 1 2 3 4	0 1 2 3 4	0 1 2 3 4
(b) New Crockery	0 1 2 3 4	0 1 2 3 4	0 1 2 3 4	0 1 2 3 4	0 1 2 3 4	0 1 2 3 4
(c) Cleaning Materials	0 1 2 3 4	0 1 2 3 4	0 1 2 3 4	0 1 2 3 4	0 1 2 3 4	0 1 2 3 4
(d) New Clothes for Residents	0 1 2 3 4	0 1 2 3 4	0 1 2 3 4	0 1 2 3 4	0 1 2 3 4	0 1 2 3 4
(e) New Shoes for Residents	0 1 2 3 4	0 1 2 3 4	0 1 2 3 4	0 1 2 3 4	0 1 2 3 4	0 1 2 3 4
(f) New Furniture	0 1 2 3 4	0 1 2 3 4	0 1 2 3 4	0 1 2 3 4	0 1 2 3 4	0 1 2 3 4
(g) New Appliances TV, Radio, Refrig.	0 1 2 3 4	0 1 2 3 4	0 1 2 3 4	0 1 2 3 4	0 1 2 3 4	0 1 2 3 4

(h) Food Supplies	0	0	0	0	0	0
other than	1	1	1	1	1	1
meals	2	2	2	2	2	2
	3	3	3	3	3	3
	4	4	4	4	4	4

14. If an electrical appliance needs fixing in one of your buildings, how are arrangements made for this to be done. (Probe who involved.)

15. If repair to furniture is necessary in any of your buildings, how is this done. (Probe who involved.)

16. What arrangements are made for laundry of (a) sheets & towels, (b) resident clothes in your buildings.

16a. How are the numbers of staff assigned to your buildings determined.

17. Do you meet with any of the direct care personnel in your buildings.

                                        Yes

                                        No

18. If yes to Question 17, how often do you do this and who comes to the meetings.

                    Daily......................
                    Weekly.....................
                    Monthly....................
                    Less often than monthly.....
                    Other......................

19. What do you discuss at these meetings.

20. When was the last time you met with direct care staff in each of your buildings. Who was present.

Building   Date of Last Meeting   Staff Present

_____

_____

_____

_____

_____

_____

21. Do you meet with any of the following assigned to your Unit.   How often.

			Frequency
Physicians	Yes	No	
Social Workers	Yes	No	
Psychologists	Yes	No	
O.T.'s	Yes	No	
P.T.'s	Yes	No	
Rehab.	Yes	No	
Teachers	Yes	No	
Others	Yes	No	
Nurses			

22. When was the last time you met with any of those people attached to your Unit, was any one else present?

	Date	Other Staff Present
Physicians		
Social Workers		
Psychologists		
O.T.'s		
P.T.'s		
Rehab.		
Teachers		

	Date	Other Staff Present

Others _____

Nurses _____

23. Do you meet with Heads of Departments.   Yes   No

24. How often does this happen.

_____

25. What is discussed at these meetings.

26. Do you meet with the Superintendent.   Yes   No

27. If yes to Question 26, how often does this happen and what do you discuss.

    Frequency: _____

    Topic:

28. Do you meet with any of the 3 assistant superintendents.

            All .... Yes   No
            2 .... Yes   No
            1 ... . Yes   No

29. If yes to Question 28, how often do you do this and what do you discuss.

                    Frequency   Topic

    1st AS _____

    2nd AS _____

    3rd AS _____

30. Who decides when direct care staff have their days off in your buildings.
    (Probe who, final say.)
    Building

    _____
    _____
    _____
    _____
    _____

31. Who decides when direct care staff have their vacations in your buildings.
    (Probe who, final say.)

    <u>Building</u>

    _____

    _____

    _____

    _____

    _____

    _____

32. Who decides what tasks the direct care staff will do in your buildings.
    (Probe who, final say.)

    <u>Building</u>

    _____

    _____

    _____

    _____

    _____

    _____

33. Who decides the times the residents get up in your buildings.

    <u>Building</u>

    _____

    _____

    _____

    _____

    _____

    _____

34 Who decides the times the residents go to bed in your buildings.

    <u>Building</u>

    _____

    _____

    _____

35. Who decides the time of meals in your buildings.

Building

_____

_____

_____

_____

_____

_____

36. Do you have programmes for individual residents in any of your buildings.
    Which buildings, how many residents

Building   Number

_____

_____

_____

_____

_____

_____

37. If yes to Question 36, who is involved in planning these activities.

Building   Personnel

_____

_____

_____

_____

_____

_____

38. Who decides when residents should be transferred to other buildings?

Building   Personnel

_____

_____

_____

_____

_____

38a. Who decides when residents should be discharged?

Building   Personnel

_____

_____

_____

_____

_____

38b. Who decides when residents should be placed in programmes outside the building

Building   Personnel

_____

_____

_____

_____

_____

39. Who decides when a resident should be admitted to your buildings.

Building   Personnel

_____

_____

_____

_____

40. Who decides when a resident can go on home leave in your buildings.

Building   Personnel

_____

_____

_____

_____

_____

_____

41. Do you have a petty cash allowance for any of your buildings.

Yes

No   Number of buildings   _____

42. To whom do you see yourself as directly answerable.

43. Do you have to make reports to this person, are they written or verbal,
    and how often are they given.

44. What would you see as being the ends to which you are working in each
    of the buildings in your Unit?

Building

_____

_____

_____

_____

_____

_____

Interviewee

Name _____

Title _____

Department _____

Date _____

Interviewer _____

_____

DEPARTMENT HEAD INTERVIEW

1. Could you start by telling me briefly what are the primary goals of your
    Department and what are the main problems which you encounter in trying
    to achieve them?

2(a) What is the title of your position? _____

 (b) Is this a full time or part time position?　　FT

　　　　　　　　　　　　　　　　　　　　　　　　　　　PT

 (c) How long have you been in this position? _____

 (d) What was your last educational or
     professional qualification?　　_____

3. Who are you responsible to for your work?

4. Do you provide him (them) with any written
    reviews of your activities?　　Yes

　　　　　　　　　　　　　　　　　　　　No

5. (If yes) How often is this done? _____

6. How many personnel are there working
    in your department at the moment?　　N - _____

7. Do you have any vacancies at the moment?
    (If yes) How many?　　N - _____

8. Are any of your blocks being used in other
    departments at the moment?
    (If yes) How many?　　N - _____

9. Is your department formally divided into
    sub-departments?   Yes

    (If no, go to Q.12)   No

10. Can you tell me what these sub-departments are called, who is in charge
    of each and how many personnel are currently working in each?

Sub-Department Name	Sub-Department Head	N Personnel

11. Does each of these sub-departments provide you with written reviews of their
    activities or is this done verbally?

    (a) all provide written reviews

    (b) some written, some verbal

    (c) all verbal

    (comments)

Now I want to ask a few questions about who has the authority to make certain decisions affecting your department(s). In each case I would like to know who normally has the authority to make the decision.

12. Who has the authority to decide

    (a) the numbers of staff allocated to your department(s) _____

          _____

    (b) who is hired to fill a position in your
        department(s)? _____

          _____

    (c) whether a person in your department(s)
        is to be fired? _____

          _____

    (d) what tasks people in your department(s)
        work on? _____

          _____

13. Do you have written procedures governing the day-to-day work which your subordinates do?

    (a) yes, for all or most aspects of work

    (b) for some aspects of work

    (c) for few or no aspects of work

14. Now could you tell me what are the main committees or other regular meetings which you take part in at the school. Please tell me who else attends and how often the meetings take place? (If unclear, ask what it does)

Committee Meeting Name and Responsibilities	Membership	Frequency

Now I want to ask you some questions about unitisation and the units.

15. Do you have any written document specifying the relationship of your department(s) to the units?

Yes

No

16. Are any of your staff formally assigned to units?

(If no, go to Q.22)

Yes

No

17. As I go through a list of the units can you tell me how many staff are assigned to each?

Units		N of Staff
_____	....	_____
_____	....	_____
_____	....	_____
_____	....	_____
_____	....	_____
_____	....	_____
_____	....	_____
_____	....	_____

18. Who has the authority to decide what work they do in the units?

_____

_____

19. Who has the authority to decide when they do their work in the units?

_____

_____

20(a) Do you have any written document specifying who has authority over these activities?

Yes

No

(b) Are they given any written procedures governing the work they do there?

Yes

No

21. Do any of these staff regularly work

(a) weekends? How many?   N - _____

(b) evenings? How many?   N - _____

22(a) Aside from the regular meetings which we've already discussed, do
you meet with any of the unit directors individually?

Yes

No

(b) (If yes) As I go through the list could you tell me roughly how often
you meet with each?

	At least weekly	At least monthly	Less often	Never
Dr Anderson				
Mr Moore				
Mrs Sellinger				
Mr Hanley				
Mr Gendron				
Mrs Fenillo				
Mr Shaw				
Mr McDade				

23. Do you keep any of your records on a unit basis

All

Most

Some

None

24. Overall, how would you rate the co-ordination of the activities of your
department(s) with the units?

(comments)

Good

Fair

Poor

25. Has unitisation made a significant difference to the activities of
     your department(s)?

     Major (redefinition of department's activities).......

     Some difference ....

     Little or none ... .

     (comments)

26   Has unitisation made a significant difference to the activities in your
     own job?

     Major (redefined or created) ....

     Some difference ....

     Little or none ....

26(a)In every kind of organisation people run into problems.   Could you say
     what you find to be the main problems in your job.

26(b)Are there any things you would like to see changed here.

27. Finally, are there any other important issues which we haven't discussed
     about the operation of your department(s) and its (their) relation to
     other areas of the school?

```
                                          Interviewee _____

                                          Interviewer _____

                                          Date        _____

                                          Time: Start _____

                                                Finish _____
```

SENIOR ADMINISTRATION INTERVIEW

1. Could you tell me briefly what are your primary goals or objectives for the
    school?

2. What are the major problems which you encounter in trying to achieve these?

3. (a) Is your position as (Asst.) Superintendent: <u>full</u> <u>time</u> or <u>part</u> <u>time</u>?

   (b) How long have you been in your present position?

4. In this capacity, roughly what percentage of your time can you give to long-
    term planning as opposed to day-to-day problems?

            per cent of time   _____ (a) long-term planning

                                  _____ (b) day-to-day problems

5. Similarly, how is your time divided between people who work inside the
    school and people who work outside?

            per cent of time   _____ (a) inside

                                  _____ (b) outside

6. Who are you responsible to for your work?

7. (a) Do you provide him/them with any written
        reviews of your activities?   Yes   No

    (b) (If yes) How often is this done?   _____

8. Which departments are directly responsible to you?   Can you tell me the name
    of the departments and the name of the person in charge of each?   (List
    under 9 below.)

9. (a) Does each of these departments provide you with a written review of
       their activities, or is this information obtained verbally?

   (b) (Ask if "some") Which do this?

Department	Head	Written Review (Write all, none, or check as appropriate)

10. Could you list for me the main committees or other regular meetings which you
    take part in at the school?   Please tell me who else attends and how often
    the meetings take place?   (If unclear, ask what it does)

Committee/Meeting Name and Responsibilities	Membership	Frequency

Turning now to problems of co-ordinating various activities in the school ...

11. How would you rate the co-ordination between:

	Good	Average	Poor

(a) the professional departments and the units?

(b) the service departments and the units?

(c) the administration and the units?

(d) the overall co-ordination of the school's
    activities?

Comments (if any)

I now want to ask who has the authority to make various decisions in the school.
In each case, I would like to know who normally can decide these things. (It
may be an individual, a position, or a committee.)

12. Who has the authority to decide on the contents of the budget submitted to
    the legislature?

13. Within the current budget who has the authority to decide how to allocate
    attendant blocks to the various units?

14. Who has the authority to decide how to allocate funds in the school from
    the current budget?

15. What sources of funds are there other than those allocated by the state?
    Who can authorise the spending of each of these funds?

Funds	Authority

16. Who has the authority to hire (a) heads of departments, (b) other personnel in the following areas?

	(a) Heads	(b) Other Personnel
Professional Departments		
Service Departments		
The Units		

17. Who has the authority to fire (a) heads of departments, and (b) other personnel in the same areas?

	(a) Heads	(b) Other Personnel
Professional Departments		
Service Departments		
The Units		

18. Who has the authority to admit a new resident?

19. Who has the authority to discharge a resident?

20. Who has the authority to transfer a resident from one unit to another?

21. Do you have any written policies about resident care?   yes   no

22. To whom are these made available?

23. By whom were they prepared?

Turning to Unitisation _per se_ ...

24. First could you tell me where and when the decision to unitise was made? (Probe - were you involved in the decision?)

25. At this stage would you say that unitisation is

   (a) virtually complete?   (If (a) go to 27)

   (b) only partially complete?

26. (a) What aspects are complete?

   (b) What remains to be done?

27. (a) Is there any written plan for unitisation at your school?

   (b) To whom is it made available?

   (c) By whom was it prepared?

   (d) Can I see a copy?

28. Has unitisation made specific differences to your own job in terms of either relieving you of some activities which you used to perform or adding new activities to your job?

   (a) activities no longer performed

   (b) additional activities

29. Overall, what is your assessment of the value of unitisation to your school so far?

Turning to relationships between the school and its environment ...

30. What external groups or agencies do you have to deal with? (List under 32 below)

31. Do you attend any regular meetings with these? How often? (List under 32 below)

32. Do you provide any of them with written reports? How often?

Group/Agency	Meeting (Frequency)	Reports (Frequency)

33. What are the major problems that arise in dealing with these groups and agencies?

34. What, if any, major changes have occurred in the last 5 years in dealing with these outside agencies and groups?

35. To what extent do you feel that these agencies and groups constrain or restrict what you can do in the school?   (greatly, moderately, little)

36. Finally, are there any other important aspects of the school and your job which we haven't discussed?   (e.g. are you concentrating on any particular areas at the moment?)

APPENDIX II. SCALES AND INDICES

Revised Resident Management Practices Scale

1. Do the residents get up at the same time on weekends as they do during the week?

2. Do the residents go to bed at the same time on weekends as they do during the week?

3. When may residents use the yard?

4. When may residents use their bedrooms?

5. When may visitors come?

6. Are any residents toileted at night?

7. What do the residents do between dressing and breakfast?

8. Do the residents wait in line before breakfast?

9. Do residents wait in a group before bathing?

10. Do residents wait in a group after bathing?

11. How do residents return from the toilet?

12. How long do residents wait at table before meal is served?

13. How long do residents wait at table after meal is served?

14. How are residents organised when they go on walks?

15. What is done with clothing a resident brings?

16. What is done with the personal possessions a resident brings with him?

17. How many residents possess all of the following items of clothing: shirt or blouse; trousers or skirts; dress or jacket; sweater; top coat; shoes; bathrobe; slippers?

18. Where are the residents' daily clothes kept?

19. How many residents have personal possessions?

20. Are residents allowed pictures and pinups in their rooms?

21. How are the residents' birthdays celebrated?

22. How are tables set for meals?

23. How many residents can use the kitchen?

24. Do the residents have access to the office?

25. How do staff assist residents at showering time?

26. Do staff on duty eat with the residents?

27. Do staff on duty watch television with residents?

28. How many residents have been on outings in the last three months?

APPENDIX 2:2

INDEX OF PHYSICAL ENVIRONMENT

Item No.   Content

1 .... Ratio of bathrooms to residents

2 .... Ratio of handbasins to residents

3 .... Ratio of tubs/showers to residents

4 .... % of showers with partitions and doors

5 .... Ratio of mirrors to residents

6 .... % of bathrooms with mirrors

7 .... % of toilets with paper

8 .... % of toilets partitioned

9 .... % of toilets with doors

10 .... Ratio of dorms to residents

11 .... % of residents with lockers

12 .... % of residents with own closets

13 .... % of residents with bed drawers

14 .... % of dorms with posters

15 .... % of dorms with curtains and shades

16 .... % of dorms with mirrors

17 .... Ratio of TV's and radios

18 .... Ratio of armchairs and settees

19 .... Ratio of occasional tables

20 .... % of bookshelves with toy cupboards

21 .... % of dayrooms with curtains or shades

22 .... % of dayrooms with waste bins

Scoring Procedures

Ratio Scales					Percentage Scales		

<table>
<tr><td colspan="3">Ratio Scales</td><td></td><td colspan="2">Percentage Scales</td></tr>
<tr><td>1 : 1 - 1:2</td><td>=</td><td>0</td><td></td><td>100-80</td><td>= 0</td></tr>
<tr><td>1 : 3 - 1:5</td><td>=</td><td>1</td><td></td><td>60-79</td><td>= 1</td></tr>
<tr><td>1 : 5 - 1:10</td><td>=</td><td>2</td><td></td><td>40-59</td><td>= 2</td></tr>
<tr><td>1 : 11 - 1:15</td><td>=</td><td>3</td><td></td><td>20-39</td><td>= 3</td></tr>
<tr><td>1 : 16</td><td>=</td><td>4</td><td></td><td>0-19</td><td>= 4</td></tr>
</table>

Appendix 2:3

Index of Community Involvement

1. How many residents went shopping in the last month?

2. How many residents went to the cinema in the last month?

3. How many residents went to a museum in the last month?

4. How many residents have been on a public bus in the last month?

5. How many residents have been to a restaurant or a cafeteria in the last month?

6. How many residents went to a house other than that of their parents for a visit in the last month?

7. How many residents have been for a car ride in the last month?

8. How many residents have been to religious services off the grounds in the last month?

9. How many residents have been on overnight visits home or elsewhere in the last month?

10. How many residents have been to a hairdresser in the last month?

11. How many residents have been to a doctor or dentist off the grounds in the last month?

12. How many residents went on a vacation in the last year with their family?

13. How many residents went on a vacation organised by the school or other in the last year?

Scoring Procedure

100–80%	=	0
60–79%	=	1
40–59%	=	2
20–39%	=	3
0–19%	=	4

INDEX OF BUILDING SUPERVISORS' PARTICIPATION IN DECISION-MAKING

1. Who is usually involved in deciding the time the residents get up in your residence?

2. Who is usually involved in deciding the times the residents go to bed in your residence?

3. Who is usually involved in deciding on the admission of a resident to your residence?

4. Who is usually involved in deciding when a resident should be discharged from your residence?

5. Who is usually involved in deciding when a resident can go on home leave?

6. Who is usually involved in hiring new attendants for your residence?

7. Who is usually involved in firing attendants in your residence?

8. Who is usually involved in deciding when attendants have their days off in your residence?

9. Who is usually involved in deciding when attendants take their vacations in your residence?

10. Who is usually involved in planning programmes for residents in your residence?

SCORING PROCEDURE

0 = Building supervisor makes the decision without consulting a superior but may consult with subordinates.

1 = Building supervisor is _always_ consulted by a superior.

2 = Building supervisor is _sometimes_ consulted by a superior.

3 = The issues are always decided by a superior or professional and the building supervisor is _not_ involved in making the decision, _or_ rules exist to determine what will happen.

BIBLIOGRAPHY

Aiken, M. & Hage, J. (1966). 'Organizational alienation: a comparative analysis', *American Sociological Review*, vol. 31, 497-507.

Alutto, T. & Acito, F. (1973). 'Decisional participation and sources of job satisfaction', unpublished thesis, University of New York at Buffalo.

Balla, D.A. (1976).'Relationship of institution size to quality of care: a review of the literature', *American Journal of Mental Deficiency*, vol. 81, 117-24.

Bayley, N., Rhodes, L., Gooch, B. & Marcus, M. (1971). 'Environmental factors in the development of institutionalised children', in J. Hellmuth (ed.), *Exceptional Infant* (Brunner-Mazel, New York), 450-72.

Belknap, I. (1956). *Human Problems in a State Mental Hospital* (McGraw-Hill, New York).

Blatt, B. (1969). 'Purgatory', in R.B. Kugel & W. Wolfensberger (eds), *Changing Patterns in Residential Services for the Mentally Retarded* (Residential Committee on Mental Retardation, Washington, DC), 35-49.

Blatt, B. & Kaplan, F. (1966). *Christmas in Purgatory* (Allyn & Bacon, Boston, Massachusetts).

Blau, P.M. (1970). 'Decentralisation in bureaucracies', in M.N. Zald (ed.), *Power in Organizations* (Vanderbilt University Press, Nashville), 150-74.

Blindert, H.D. (1975). 'Interactions between residents and staff', *Mental Retardation*, vol. 13, 38-40.

Bogdan, R., Taylor, S., DeGrandpre, B. & Haynes, S. (1974). 'Let them eat programs: attendants' perspectives and programming on wards in State schools', *Journal of Health and Social Behaviour*, vol. 15, 142-51.

Butterfield, E.C. (1968). 'The characteristics, selection and training of institutional personnel', in A.A. Baumeister (ed.), *Mental Retardation: appraisal, education and rehabilitation* (University of London Press, London), 305-28.

Butterfield, E.C., Barnett, C.D. & Bensberg, G.J. (1966). 'Some objective characteristics of institutions for the mentally retarded: implications for attendant turnover rate', *American Journal of Mental Deficiency*, vol. 70, 786-94.

Butterfield, E.C. & Warren, S.A. (1962). 'The use of the M.M.P.I. in the selection of hospital aides', *Journal of Applied Psychology*, vol. 46, 34-40.

—— (1968). 'Prediction of attendant tenure', *Journal of Applied Psychology*, vol. 47, 101-3.

Caudill, W. (1958). *The Psychiatric Hospital As a Small Society* (Harvard University Press, Cambridge, Mass.).

Cleland, C.C. & Peck, R. (1959). 'Psychological determinants of tenure in institutional personnel', *American Journal of Mental Deficiency*, vol. 63, 876-88.

Commonwealth of Massachusetts Civil Service (1969). *Job Specifications*, (Boston, Massachusetts).

Dailey, W., Allen, G., Chinsky, J. & Veit, S. (1974). 'Attendant behaviour and attitudes toward institutionalised retarded children', *American Journal of Mental Deficiency*, vol. 78, 586-91.

Department of Health and Social Security (1969). *Report of the Committee of Inquiry into allegations of ill-treatment of patients and other irregularities at the Ely Hospital, Cardiff* (HMSO, London).

—— (1977). 'The facilities and services of mental illness and mental handicap hospitals in England, 1975' in *Statistical and Research Report Series No. 19* (HMSO, London).

English, H.N. (1964). 'A state hospital moves into community mental health services', *Mental Hospitals*, vol. 15, 698-700.

Etzioni, A. (1960). 'Interpersonal and structural factors in the study of mental hospitals', *Psychiatry*, vol. 23, 13-22.

Farrell, M.J. & Moser, H.W. (1969). *Unitization at Fernald: A Preliminary Proposal* (mimeographed, Waltham, Massachusetts).

Fishbein, M. & Ajzen, L. (1974). 'Attitudes toward objects as predictors of single and multiple behavioural criteria', *Psychological Review*, vol. 81, 59-74.

Fleming, J.W. (1962). 'The critical incidence technique as an aid to in-service training', *American Journal of Mental Deficiency*, vol. 67, 41-52.

Goffman, E. (1961). *Asylums* (Doubleday, New York).

Grant, G.W.B. & Moores, B. (1977). 'Resident characteristics and staff behaviour in two hospitals for the mentally-retarded', *American Journal of Mental Deficiency*, vol. 82, 259-65.

Greenblatt, M. & Stone, E. (1972). *Challenge and Response* (Alfred C. Holland, Boston, Mass.).

Grossman, H.J. (ed.) (1973). *Manual on Terminology and Classification in Mental Retardation* (American Association on Mental Deficiency, Washington, DC).

Grusky, O. (1959). 'Role conflict in organizations', *Administrative Science Quarterly*, vol. 3, 452-72.

Hage, J. & Aiken, M. (1967). 'Relationship of centralization to other structural properties', *Administrative Science Quarterly*, vol. 12, 72-92.

Hall, R.H. (1962). 'Intraorganizational Structural Variation', *Administrative Science Quarterly*, vol. 7, 295-308.

—— (1963). 'The concept of bureaucracy', *American Journal of Sociology*, vol. 69, 32-40.

—— (1967). 'Some organizational considerations in the professional-organizational relationship', *Administrative Science Quarterly*, vol. 12, 461-78.

Harris, J.M., Veit, S.W., Allen, G.J. & Chinsky, J.M. (1974). 'Aide-resident ratio and ward population density as mediators of social interaction', *American Journal of Mental Deficiency*, vol. 79, 320-6.

Henninger, O.P. (1963). 'The effects of the unit plan on patients and staff', in *The Unit Plan* (Mental Health Association of Southeastern Pennsylvania, Philadelphia).

Henry, J. (1954). 'The formal social structure of a psychiatric hospital', *Psychiatry*, vol. 17, 139-51.

—— (1957). 'Types of institutional structure', in M. Greenblatt (ed.), *The Patient and the Mental Hospital* (Free Press, Glencoe, Illinois), 73-90.

Holland, T. (1973). 'Organizational structure and institutional care', *Journal of Health and Social Behaviour*, vol. 14, 241-51.

Joint Commission on Accreditation of Hospitals (1971). *Standards for Residential Facilities for the Mentally Retarded* (Joint Commission for the Accreditation of Hospitals, Chicago).

Jones, K. (1975). *Opening the Door: Study of New Policies for the Mentally Retarded* (Routledge & Kegan Paul, London).

Kiger, R.S. (1966). 'Adopting the unit plan', *Hospitals and Community Psychiatry*, vol. 17, 207-10.

King, R.D. & Raynes, N.V. (1968). 'An operational measure of inmate management in residential institutions', *Social Science and Medicine*, vol. 2, 41-53.

King, R.D., Raynes, N.V. & Tizard, J. (1971). *Patterns of Residential Care* (Routledge & Kegan Paul, London).

Kushlick, A. (1975). 'Epidemiology and evaluation of services for the mentally handicapped', in M.J. Begab & S.A. Richardson (eds), *The Mentally Retarded and Society: A Social Science Perspective* (University Park Press, Baltimore), 325-43.

Kushlick, A., Blunden, R. & Cox, G.R. (1973). 'A Method of Rating Behaviour Characteristics for use in large-scale Surveys of Mental Handicap', *Psychological Medicine*, vol. 3, 466-78.

Levy, E. & McLeod, W. (1977). 'The effects of environmental design on adolescents in an institution', *Mental Retardation*, vol. 15, 28-32.

Liska, A.E. (1974). 'Emergent issues in the attitude-behaviour consistency controversy', *American Sociological Review*, vol. 39, 261-72.

McCormick, M., Balla, D. & Zigler, E. (1975). 'Resident-care practices in institutions for retarded persons: a cross-institutional, cross-cultural study', *American Journal of Mental Deficiency*, vol. 80, 1-17.

McLain, R.E., Silverstein, A.B., Hubbell, M. & Brownlee, L. (1975). 'The characterization of residential environments within a hospital for the mentally retarded', *Mental Retardation*, vol. 13, 24-7.

Massachusetts Mental Retardation Planning Project (1966). *Massachusetts Plans for its Retarded* (Commonwealth of Massachusetts, Boston).

Maxwell, A.E. (1971). *Analyzing Qualitative Data* (Methuen, London).

Milgram, S. (1965). 'Some conditions of obedience and disobedience to authority', *Human Relations*, vol. 18, 57-76.

Miller, E.J. & Gwynne, G.V. (1972). *A Life Apart* (Tavistock, London).

Millham, S.L., Bullock, R. & Cherrett, P. (1975). *After Grace — Teeth* (Chaucer, London).

Minge, M.R. & Bowman, T. (1969). 'Attendants' views of causes of short-term employment at an institution for the mentally retarded', *Mental Retardation*, vol. 7, 28-30.

Mischel, W. (1973). 'Toward a cognitive social learning reconceptualization of personality', *Psychological Review*, vol. 80, 252-83.

Moores, B. & Grant, G.W.B. (1976). 'Nurses' expectations for accomplishment of mentally retarded patients', *American Journal of Mental Deficiency*, vol. 80, 644-9.

Morris, P. (1969). *Put Away* (Routledge & Kegan Paul, London).

Nirje, B.A. (1969). 'Scandinavian visitor looks at U.S. institutions', in R.B. Kugel & W. Wolfensberger (eds), *Changing Patterns in Residential Services for the Mentally Retarded* (President's Committee on Mental Retardation, Washington, DC), 51-7.

Parnicky, J.S. & Ziegler, R.C. (1964). 'Attendant training — a national survey', *Mental Retardation*, vol. 2, 76-82.

Paulson, S.R. (1974). 'Causal analysis of inter-organisational relations: an axiomatic theory revisited', *Administrative Science Quarterly*, vol. 19, 319-37.

Perrow, C. (1972). *Complex Organizations* (Scott Foresman and Co., Glenvie Illinois).

Polsky, H.W. (1963). *Cottage Six, the Social System of Delinquent Boys in Residential Treatment* (Russel Sage Foundation, New York).

Porter, L., Lawler, E. & Hackman, J. (1975). *Behaviour in Organizations* (McGraw-Hill, New York).

Pratt, M. & Hall, W.S. (1977). *Testing for Competence: Changing the Criterion*, Working Paper, No. 4, (Laboratory of Comparative Human Cognition, Rockefeller University).

Pratt, M.W., Bumstead, D.C. & Raynes, N.V. (1976). 'Attendant staff speech to the institutionalized retarded: language use as a measure of the quality of care', *Child Psychology and Psychiatry*, vol. 17, 133-43.

Pugh, D.S., Hickson, D.J., Hinings, C.R., Macdonald, G.M., Turner, C. & Lupton, T. (1963). 'A conceptual scheme for organizational analysis', *Administrative Science Quarterly*, vol. 8, 289-315.

Pugh, D.S., Hickson, D.J., Hinings, C.R. & Turner, C. (1968). 'Dimensions of organization structure', *Administrative Science Quarterly*, vol. 13, 65-105.

Pugh, D.S., Hickson, D.J. & Hinings, C.R. (1969). 'An empirical taxonomy of structures of work organizations', *Administrative Science Quarterly*, vol. 14, 115-26.

Rapoport, R.N. (1967). *Community as Doctor* (Social Science Paperback, London).

Raynes, N.V. & King, R.D. (1968). 'The Measurement of child management in residential institutions for the retarded', in B.W. Richards (ed.), *Proceedings First Congress International Association Scientific Study of Mental Deficiency* (Michael Jackson, Surrey), 637-47.

Rokeach, M. & Klieujunas, P. (1972). 'Behaviour as a function of attitude-toward-object and attitude-toward-situation', *Journal of Personality and Social Psychology*, vol. 22, 194-201.

Salisbury, R.F. (1962). *Structures of Custodial Care, an Anthropological Study of a State Mental Hospital* (University of California Publications, Berkeley & Los Angeles).

Scheerenberger, R.C. (1965). 'A current census of state institutions for the mentally retarded', *Mental Retardation*, vol. 3, 4-6.

_____ (1976). 'A survey of public residential facilities', *Mental Retardation*, vol. 14, 32-5.

Scheff, T.J. (1961). 'Control over policy by attendants in a mental hospital', *Journal of Health and Human Behaviour*, vol. 2, 93-105.

Schein, E. (1968). 'Organizational socialization and the profession of management', *Industrial Management Review*, vol. 9, 1-16.

_____ (1971). 'The individual, the organization and the career: a conceptual scheme', *Journal of Applied Behavioural Science*, vol. 7, 401-26.

Schreiber, M. (1976). 'Unitization and social work in institutional programs for mentally retarded persons', *Mental Retardation*, vol. 14, 21-3.

Schwartz, M. (1957). 'What is a therapeutic milieu?', in M. Greenblatt,D.J. Levinson and R.H. Williams (eds), *The Patient and the Mental Hospital* (Free Press, Glencoe, Illinois).

Shearn, C.R. (1966). 'Role changes in clinical psychology following decentralization', *Journal of Clinical Psychology*, vol. 22, 341-3.

Sinclair, I.A.C. (1971). *Hostels for Probationers* (HMSO, London).

Skeels, H. (1966). *Adult Status of Children with Contrasting Early Life Experiences: a follow-up study*. Monograph No. 25 (The Society for Research in Child Development, vol. 31).

Snow, H.B. (1965). 'Aspects of decentralization of a State hospital', *Psychiatric Quarterly*, vol. 39, 607-20.

Stanton, A.H. & Schwartz, M.S. (1954). *The Mental Hospital* (Basic Books, New York).

Tannenbaum, R. & Masarik, F. (1950). 'Participation by subordinates in the managerial decision-making process', *Canadian Journal of Economics and Political Science*, vol. 16, 408-18.

Tarjan, G., Shotwell, A.M. & Dingman, H.F. (1956). 'A screening test for psychiatric technicians: continuation report on the work assignment aid, validation studies at various hospitals', *American Journal of Mental Deficiency*, vol. 60, 458-62.

Thormalen, P.W. (1965). *A Study of on-the-Ward Training of Trainable Mentally Retarded Children in a State Institution* (Sacramento, California, Department of Mental Hygiene).

Tizard, B. (1975). 'Varieties of residential nursery experience', in J. Tizard, I. Sinclair & R.V.G. Clarke (eds), *Varieties of Residential Experience* (Routledge & Kegan Paul, London), 102-21.

Tizard, B., Cooperman, O., Joseph, A. & Tizard, J. (1972). 'Environmental Effects on language development: a study of young children in long-stay residential nurseries', *Child Development*, vol. 43, 337-58.

Tizard, J. (1964). *Community Services for the Mentally Handicapped* (Oxford University Press, London).

Tizard, J., Sinclair, I. & Clarke, R.V.G. (1975). *Varieties of Residential Experience* (Routledge & Kegan Paul, London).

—— (1975). 'Introduction', in J. Tizard, I. Sinclair & R.V.G. Clarke (eds), *Varieties of Residential Experience* (Routledge & Kegan Paul, London), 1-16.

Ullman, L.P. (1967). *Institution and Outcome* (Pergamon Press, London).

Veit, S.W., Allen, G.J. & Chinsky, J.M. (1976). 'Interpersonal interactions between institutionalized retarded children and their attendants', *American Journal of Mental Deficiency*, vol. 80, 535-42.

Vroom, V.H. (1964). *Working and Motivation* (John Wiley & Sons, New York).

Williams, C. (1967). *Caring for People* (Allen & Unwin, London).

Wing, J.K. & Brown, G.W. (1970). *Institutionalism and Schizophrenia* (Cambridge University Press, London).

Wolfensberger, W. (1969). 'Twenty predictions about the future of residential services in mental retardation', *Mental Retardation*, vol. 7, 51-4.

——— (1971). 'Will there always be an institution? I.–The impact of epidemiological trends', *Mental Retardation*, vol. 9, 14-20.

Zigler, E. (1977). '20 years of mental retardation research', *Mental Retardation*, vol. 15 (3), 51-3.

Zimbardo, P., Haney, C. & Banks, W.C. (1975). 'A Prandellian Prison', in E. Krupat (ed.), *Psychology is Social* (Scott, Foresman and Co., Glenview, Illinois).

Zubowicz, G. (1967). 'The modified unit plan', *Hospital and Community Psychiatry*, vol. 18, no. 2, 44-6.

INDEX

administrators 39, *see also* department heads, unit directors, superintendents

architecture 55

attendants *see* direct-care staff

attitude-behaviour consistency 103-4

autonomy *see* centralisation

budget procedure 146-7, 155

building *see* residence

building heads 40; career ladder 61; length of service 60-1, *see also* centralisation, communication, specialisation

building heads' demographic characteristics: age 60; implications for care 156; sex 60

building heads' training 60

building matron *see* building heads

building supervisors *see* building heads

care: dimensions of 26-7; indices 32; multi-dimensionality of 14, 26, 159; variance in one institution 16, 69-70

care workers 14, *see also* building heads, direct-care staff

case studies 13

centralisation of authority 14, 36-7; building heads' perception of extent 124-5; definition 35; direct-care staff perception of extent 110; implications for care 110-11, 117, 120, 125, 136, 157-8; measures of building heads' perception 42-3, 123-5; measures of direct-care workers' perception 40, 109-10; relation to other indices of organisation structure 133-4, 158; relation to staff morale 133; reported effects in institutions for the mentally retarded 36-7

charge attendant *see* building heads

Child Management Scale 13, 14, 27; scores compared with Revised Resident Management Practices Scale scores 72-3

Commonwealth of Massachusetts 16, 19; Department of Administration and Finance 20; Department of Human Services 20; Department of Mental Health 9, 16, 19, 44; Department of Mental Health Central Office 19, 147

communication 35, 38; implications for care 117, 127-9, 134, 158; relation to other dimensions of organisational structure 134, 157-8, *see also* communication by building heads and communication by direct-care staff

communication by building heads 43, 126-9, 134, 157-8

communication by direct-care staff 40, 114-16, 121, 134

contact with surrounding community: data collection 31; frequency 81-4; implications for care 31, 83, *see* Index of Community Involvement

decentralisation of authority 35-6, 157, *see* centralisation, decentralisation of authority

decision making *see* centralisation of authority

demographic characteristics of residents *see* residents' characteristics

department heads 46, 140-1; grade levels 155; relation to unit directors 142

direct-care staff 40, 45, 54; job description 112; length of service 59; representativeness of sample 41-2, 57, *see also* centralisation, formalisation, communication, specialisation, morale, attitudes to work place

direct-care staff demographic characteristics: age 56-7; implications for care 106-8, 121, 156; sex 57-8

direct-care staff training 58-9; implications for care 107

formalisation 14, 35, 37-8; implications for care 111-14, 117; measures of direct-care workers' perception 40, 112-13; relation to other indices of organisation structure 134, 158

functional units 21, 51-3; implications for care 54, 97, 148-9, 159

Index of Community Involvement (ICI): development 31-2; effect of unit membership 81; relation to resident IQ 32, 83-4; residence scores 81; unit scores 81, *see also*